NINETY YEARS IN ONE HOUSE

Other books by Jane Hales

The East Wind (1969)
History of the Norfolk Red Cross (1970)
Three Centuries of Holt
The Norfolk Year (1970)
Looking at Norfolk (1971)
with William Bennett
Norfolk Places (1975)
Norfolk Patchwork (1979)
One Thing and Another (1982)
A Family of No Importance (1984)
Memoirs of a Modest Mountaineer (1984)
A Carousel of Nature (1985)
The Seasons of Norfolk (1988)
Norfolk Welfare - Here and There (1989)
with Shirley Warden
Blakeney Point and the Glaven Ports (1990)
with Nicholas Simms
Winds of Change in Norfolk (1991)
On the Parish (1994)

NINETY YEARS IN ONE HOUSE

JANE HALES

her last book

Larks Press

Published by the Larks Press
Ordnance Farmhouse, Guist Bottom,
Dereham NR20 5PF
01328 829207
Larks.Press@btinternet.com

August 1996

Reprinted by the copyright-owners in December 2009

and printed by Newprint and Design
Garrood Drive, Fakenham
01328 851578

British Library Cataloguing–in-Publication Data
A catalogue record for this book is available
from the British Library

ISBN 978 0 948400 47 1

PREFACE

Perhaps I am eccentric or just peculiar, but on reaching the age of 90, I have an urge to sit down and write what I remember of my long life, having lived it all in the same house. It is not because I have any claim to fame or distinction. I am a very ordinary person; my only excuse is that I have seen many changes, and it is well known that all of us are really different both mentally and physically, such is the diversity of humanity. Many have wonderful life stories to tell, but they never do so.

JANE HALES

Editor's Note

Miss Hales gave me the text of this little book shortly before she died last summer. Very little editing has been undertaken; the story is as she wrote it. I am most grateful to Mrs Ann Anderson for her help in providing the photographs.

S.Y.

The Hales Family at Holt about 1904
Behind: Father, Henry, Mother with Jane as a baby, Robert.
In front: Cousin Barbara, Frances.

NINETY YEARS IN ONE HOUSE

I have a peculiarity regarding my family. I was an after-thought, 13 years younger than my eldest brother, 10 years younger than my sister and 9 years younger than my other brother. I was born on the 9th January, 1904, and, it was said, nearly in a violet frame as my mother was a great gardener, and the nurse was not due for a fortnight. I was baptised in Holt Church in the February. At that late hour an argument was proceeding as to what I should be called, and at last it was decided on Mabel Alice Jane, after an aunt, my mother and my maternal grandmother. I was given a small prayer book with a silver cover by the other children, and an ornamented silver mug by a great uncle who had fought in the Crimea and the Indian Mutiny. He was very old and another man stood proxy for him. He had risen to be a Major-General, and when I grew up I drank out of his mug.

I remember sitting on a chair in the garden eating custard pudding. Later still I was playing on a piece of grass where there was a bed of pink carnations which attracted me. I had come through the French windows of a room which had a persian carpet, soft to my bare feet after the gravel path.

I was fond of Miss Moffat, my sister's governess in her early 'teens. She taught me to make pot-hooks and letters on a slate with a sponge attached. The best part was washing it clean. One day for some misdemeanour I was made to stand in the corner, and I licked the red wall-paper. This caused great consternation, that I might have been poisoned, but my naughtiness was forgotten when it was found that I wasn't. When she was 16 my sister was sent away to a boarding school called Eastbury. It was supposed to be a good one, and had footmen, which impressed some families. My sister was attractive looking, with a fine complexion. She was good at games, and was soon playing for the school at tennis, cricket and hockey. There were photographs taken of the girls dressed in white blouses, school ties and black skirts and stockings - so different from the games wear today.

In 1911, which was a very hot summer, King George V was crowned. I was taken to Church in the morning, which I had not bargained for, but my mother said, "You should always go to Church when the King is crowned". There was a Sports afternoon and a competition for decorated bicycles. Eve and Amy did theirs in green and yellow, but it could not wheel. The person who won the prize used red, white and blue, and it could not wheel either. "Tilting the bucket" pleased me most. A bucket was slung on a high wooden arch. It had a piece attached to the bottom with a hole in it. A man with a pole was dragged under the bucket. He tried to pass his pole through the hole. If he missed, the bucket emptied the water over him. A very dirty-looking man won. When I went to bed that night, my mother hung a Japanese lantern from my window to celebrate the day.

Sometimes I went for a walk with the maid in the afternoon. Different roads gave me different feelings. I did not like the Cromer Road, which was the beginning of suburbia, but there we met a little boy with golden red hair and his escort. My maid said, "Oh, I should like the minding of him". Very many years after, during the war, we were looking after the soldiers in the sick bay. The Medical Officer was the very same boy, now a man, with the same coloured hair. He was the son of one of the original Gresham's School housemasters, and his name was Wynn Wilson.

One day, mother took me to the School House to see Mr Howson, the Headmaster, and his two sisters. Mr Howson showed me two ties and asked what colour they were. I said, "Purple" but he replied "No, lilac" and gave me a turnip watch on a chain. I was delighted. It was just what I had wanted. When I was a bit older, I went to the School swimming baths to learn to swim with other children and their mothers. I had a pair of blue wings to keep me afloat. When I had swum a breadth, I was to have a Boy Scout's water bottle. The water in the baths was very cold, as it was opened several weeks before the warmth of the sun had taken the chill off.

2

Holt

People mostly pass through Holt without stopping on their way from the Midlands and the South to the coast; others have heard of it in one manner and another, and come here to be in the midst of rural England. For the countryside is becoming more and more devastated by urban and suburban spread, and North Norfolk is comparatively out of the tract of this insidious creep of bricks and mortar. Long may it remain so!

But the town of Holt is no sluggish backwater. The High Street runs from the Obelisk Plain at the west end to the Market Place at the east. There are Georgian houses on either side, for there was a great fire on May Day 1708. Much of the town was burned and then rebuilt in this seemly fashion. Now Holt is designated a Conservation Area, and overhead wires have come down, and the place looks even better. The Market Place was used for its rightful purpose until the end of the last century; then the market was held behind the Feathers Hotel till it closed in 1960 - after some 900 years. In the middle of the Market Place stands the War Memorial, the design of which was taken from Binham preaching cross (Binham is a village on the road from Holt to Wells, notable for its ruined priory). Parallel to part of the High Street is Bull Street and at the western end of it is the Shirehall, with a mounting block outside. Between the two roads is Fish Hill, and its tall steep-roofed houses to which pigeons cling.

Although the Church suffered so severely from the town fire of 1708, it probably contains the oldest stone of any building in Holt. In the tower are fragments of carr-stone, a ginger-coloured variety of sandstone found in West Norfolk. Probably these pieces are of Saxon origin; although no church at Holt is mentioned in the Domesday survey, there was almost certainly one here. For the market being then in existence, people who came to it are almost sure to have had a church to attend. When Kerrich, an authority on architecture, visited Holt church in 1821, he wrote, "This of little consequence, lowness and clumsiness forms its character, and that character runs through every part, so we may say it has at least the merit of uniformity . . Mem. never go there again". Kerrich must have been feeling out of sorts that day. The building does not compare with the magnificent churches of Cley, Salthouse, and Blakeney, but it is the most distinguished edifice in Holt; within its walls for centuries, the splendid words of the Authorised Version have inspired congregations, an influence both on spirit and speech. The churchyard springs to life each year with snowdrops, crocuses, and daffodils. Between the avenue of limes, the eighteenth-century blue-faced clock shows upon the church tower. It has but one hand, so the exact time is uncertain, a comfort to the little girl and her mother who were always late for Morning Prayer.

The child sees and feels about things in a special way - we are several persons in a lifetime. To a child, local roads had their several characters and shed a different atmosphere. One was dull, almost grim, leading on and on between hedges, across empty fields; another was friendly and endearing, the sandy verge had a grass path, and ran up-and-down the bank, wide enough for a child to run along. There were sheltering woods to the east, then heath to the top of the hill, where the road rushed down to the bridge over the stream, and up again to a plantin'. Near the hill top by Burton's Cottage, was the milestone 'Norwich 20', so the length of a mile fixed itself into the child's head. This way was called the Edgefield Road for in those immobile days Norwich was too far away to be reckoned with. Altogether, the child went home with a satisfied feeling after walking upon that road. It was top of the list.

Westward, into the afternoon glare, was another dusty way. It crossed the railway bridge, and the opening to the old road which the line had stopped. The hedges were still in place, and there were two white gates on either side of the line. People talked of the old stretch of road in a familiar manner - everything interesting seemed to have happened long before the child's time. So the westward road lolloped on, by an isolated garden, secret, behind high hedges, and without a house to keep it company. Then there were the Field Houses, a line of old low dwellings, for here had been the Open Fields of the parish. The road wound down a slope to the Lime Kiln, white and dusty. Nearby was a milestone 'Dereham 18'. Dereham sounded a nice place, soft and mild.

4

The road out of the market town to the east was at the bottom of the list. Pompous Victorian villas reared up, seeming to snub the child; here were the new school buildings, but not so new as the child, and a deceiving milestone which indicated five furlongs to the town. Altogether, the road gave an uneasy feeling. Where the several roads led to in the blue distance was terra incognita.

Besides the main roads there were byways over stiles where ancient ploughs nestled in the undergrowth. The 'Candlestick' was dull but mercifully short. Then there was the long, long lane that never seemed to end. The child on the donkey was alone when the animal saw a succulent patch of grass; his head went down and the saddle slipped off. But the rider did not stay on the ground long. Walter, who had been lagging behind thinking of the parlour-maid, arrived to pick her up, replace the saddle, and tighten the girths.

Beaches had similar feelings attached to them. The shingle bank where waves burst with a constant roar sent one home rather weary and awe-inspired. But there was a strange house on the pebbles which always tickled up interest. 'Rocket Apparatus' was painted on the door. Further east was a sandy beach, the official 'sea-side' where there was plenty of room to make castles till high tide lapped the promenade. The child was puzzled as to how the breakwaters broke the waves, a question never satisfactorily answered. But westward was that magical shore beyond the marsh - the dunes and the great sands. On the far side of the lagoon, a man with a gun was walking upon a ridge of sand, but the child was not allowed to go there - too dangerous, there might be quick-sands, or you might be cut off by the tide! That brilliant place of desire in the blue seas was relegated to that seemingly unattainable time - 'when you grow up'.

In the winter there were dancing classes in a Cromer hotel. Mr Winter's Prep School also attended, and we danced the polka, the waltz and the Lancers. The girls played with balls and skipped while the boys looked on. I had a daily governess called Eva but for some unknown reason I called her Amy and she did not object. She took me once a week by the Midland and Great Northern Railway to Melton Constable and then by horse drawn vehicle to Melton Constable Hall for dancing classes. They were not so much fun as those at Cromer.

The Surgery

I saw little of my father when I was a young child as after his rounds of patients he used to have his tea sitting alone in the library, in winter before a large fire, with his hands turned up to the flames and his dogs on the rug. By dinner time I was in bed, and I did not come down to the meal till I was sixteen.

In after years I heard of what went on in the surgery from those who attended there. It was a fair sized room with a table near the window, a counter fitted with a bench and rows of shelves filled with bottles. The room was heated by an open fire, a couple of dogs before it, and near the corner a white cockatoo with a yellow plume perched in a cage. When the bird screamed, William Daddy, the dispenser, would poke it with the wooden part of a pen. Then there was a small consulting room used occasionally for special patients.

Patients came from far and wide, especially on Friday, market day. They tied their donkeys or ponies, which had drawn their carts, to the wall of the back drive or leaned their bicycles there. Some arrived on foot. My father, in a dressing gown after his bath, sat at the table

Jane's father, Dr Hales

6

listening to the patients' ailments, and in between times, accusing Daddy of all and sundry misdemeanours. Daddy would get redder in the face, and the line of patients would snigger and laugh out loud, knowing it untrue but thinking it a joke. So the entertainment continued till most of the patients had left feeling better from the laughter than there were likely to feel from a bottle of physic. There was no having to go to a chemist those days, all was done by the dispenser, even to the making of pills.

When the surgery was nearly empty, my father would get up and go into the stable and cut firewood with a strange looking Swiss saw. Doctor Daddy, as the dispenser was called, prescribed for the patients that remained, giving them mostly bottles of 'White Mixture'. He also made 'Physics'. Some was poured in a glass, a powder added and it bubbled up, and tasted nice, and was said to cure any headache or other small ailment. Anyhow, it did no harm.

After dressing, my father would either go on his rounds in gig or dog-cart with the coachman, Alfred Bacon, driving, or walk up Holt High Street with his ivory-headed stick and trail of dogs. He would shout greetings to people on the opposite side of the street, and bellow about what he thought was wrong and what he thought of somebody. Two of his special bugbears were Norwich City Football Club, because it was professional sport, and the Gresham's School, then called the Grammar School, which he thought had usurped the local boys' privileges. Strangers would ask sometimes why he was not had up for slander, to be told, 'That's only Doctor Bob'.

When William Daddy retired, a female dispenser was engaged. She told me that if an accident was brought in, my father would stitch up a wound without what she considered due precautions, but it would always heal at the first intent. My father did not charge for his services if he thought the patient would have difficulty in paying. As he grew older, his dispenser, who sent out the bills, had great difficulty in finding out whom he had seen. He seemed to think it immoral to charge for his skills. Perhaps he thought his work was on a par with water divining, and he had no right to take any money for it. He was a compassionate man.

My father never drank whisky or smoked, after having 'flu in 1914.

7

He had a reflecting candle stick by his bed (there was no electricity in the house). He would wake during the night, drink a glass of cold milk, and read Chaucer in the original. He was born in 1853 and died at the age of 77 in 1931 after a long illness. His widow put a window in Holt Church depicting the Canterbury Pilgrims. One figure in the window was that of Alfred Bacon the coachman, who had been with my grandfather.

Nowadays, as far as I know, a local doctor never contemplates operating in his own surgery, but sends the patient to a hospital; but I think my father must have had a mistrust of any but the great London hospitals. An old man at Gunthorpe told me how Doctor Bob took out an appendix on the kitchen table of a farmouse there. His friend, Doctor Harry Skrimshire of Holt gave the anaesthetic, and the patient completely recovered.

From a very early age I was taken to the Walnut Tree Farm at Edgefield in the donkey cart to see old Tom Potter and his daughter. The donkey, Patrick, was the best of his kind, and stood by the tree without being tied up. (Now some Philistine has cut it down). We had tea in the old house. The bread and butter always tasted much nicer than at home. Tom was an old retired farmer with white whiskers. There was a big kitchen leading out of the parlour with an open fireplace; by it was a door opening onto a staircase, to a room without a window, probably blocked at the time of the window tax. I was not allowed to go up the stairs, as they were rotten. Mary told me that when her mother was alive, a man used to put a 'faggot', a bundle of wood on the fire for cooking. The floor was strewn with sand, a dirty practice, she thought.

In another far-gone picture, I remember Mary showing me a spring at the corner of a field. Years after, curiosity made me go and look for it, and there it was.When I was about four, Mary married a school teacher and went to a special school for boys at Brancaster. Mary had had teacher training. All I remember of the wedding, for I was a bridesmaid, was the photograph taken outside the house. Tom had a housekeeper, and went out shooting at the age of 96.

The scenes and delights of childhood are never lost. Stored in the

8

*Frances (seated on the donkey) and Jane with
Mary Potter their governess*

mysterious recesses of the mind, they emerge in dreams; the light is
clearer, the glades softer, the grass greener, and the old houses more
welcoming. Primitive people are said to send their messages by dreams.
With childhood long gone, I had a waking dream: I was galloping
Patrick the donkey across the common, which was quite the wrong
thing to do. Somehow or other he managed shake himself free of the
cart and go off, and the worried dreamer looked for him in vain. The
next day I went to see Mary, now in a Home and a widow, and in the
course of conversation repeated the dream. Mary smiled. 'I can tell you
what happened to the donkey,' she said, 'for I too had a waking dream.
He came into the yard as I was standing by my old home, harness
hanging loose, and he was very distressed. I had to comfort him.'

In summer I used to be taken to play on the sands at Sheringham,
which was then quite a small town. On the esplanade were donkeys and
goat carts. I did not enjoy riding in a goat cart, but it pleased the
adults. Often I was taken for afternoon walks in Holt. There was a
popular walk called the Spout Hills, where water gushed out of the
slope, in a fine stream. There were often other dogs there, and some
fights which I enjoyed.

9

'Time gone by, most yards had a hay-loft, and I used mine for corn as well, but there's only a water-tank there now, and empty sacks, and odds and ends,' said the farmer. One day, no doubt, when there is no more pressing job, those odds and ends will be sorted out, and most of them consigned to the scrap heap.

Throwing away can become a compulsive passion. In rash moments, we become infected with a burning desire to clear out cupboards and junk rooms wherein inoffensive objects have lain for years, doing nobody any harm. But certainly the loft is an untidy place, boards foul with a mixture of dust and fragmented straw. It is chilly up there with only a small unglazed window and light which trickles through tiles. The shoots in the floor down to the stable below are hung with cobwebs and festooned with ancient feed. In this forlorn place is a pram, old and dejected, coal scuttles and pails rusted through, garden frames with most of the lights out, pieces of iron and wood, and 'them things which belong to the hens', troughs, and a patent water container. This junk must be got rid of, so one day a lorry is driven into the cobbled yard, and the swing hatch in the wall of the loft is opened sending in a flood of light.

First, the pram is bundled down into the open vehicle with gusto, and much else besides, but not everything is sent into oblivion. The cleaner has just enough sense left to save a roll of stout wire and the poultry utensils, for, as her companion remarks, 'they 'ould be really dear ter buy in the shop, nartin' don't come down ter day only the rain!' The cleaner has a bit of sentiment left, and puts the big bell on its spring aside, 'what had fetched 'em in from the garden'. Later, she hangs it by the back door of the house across the yard, for it will be handy for callers when the electric bell is sulky. Also, she saves the pair of clogs with leathers up to the knee, for she can still hear them, through the years, being stumped over the cobbles by the coachman washing a carriage.

A couple of side-saddles are in a corner. One of them is quite heavy to move, and the other has a stitched leather seat beneath the dust, and both have their padding torn. They are taken into the yard and polished up a bit. A friend says side-saddles are scarce, and these should be worth a lot of money, but somebody else declares they had better be put in the lorry with the rest of the junk. In the end, they are sold, for a modest sum to the museum-keeper of the local saddlery. There they will be on show, clean and shining, harness of antiquity to be wondered at, and the clogs are there too. The cleaner leaves a toboggan in the loft for it may come in useful to bring shopping home when the snow is deep in the Street. She finds a queer iron contraption, its use beyond memory, and that is left for further inspection.

Through in the granary, Biddell's Patent Oats and Beans Cutter remains standing, and there is a hay-cutter bolted to the floor. Part of a canopy bedstead leans against the wall; that must stay, it is too big and awkward to get out.

Rooms and buildings go out of fashion, or lose their significance. The back-'us is no longer mentioned, and the back-'us boy is quite extinct. The knife-house in the yard below the loft has gone except for the brick floor, and a cotoneaster is growing there. It was a small place with a shelf and smooth board upon, reddened with powder, on which dinner knives were cleaned - no blunt stainless steel then! The great dog kennel has gone too. In forgotten time, a half-mythical dog must have slept inside, but afterwards it was a retreat for bantams (the cocks fought fiercely and had to be revived with whisky). Within the stables the harness room is dilapidated, the green baize on the walls in tatters. The loose-boxes are full of logs and coal and in one of them is a piece of furniture being stored for somebody or other. The handle of the pump near the loft ladder is limp and sends no water on to the grating beneath.

Years roll back in the mind's eye. A wagon load of straw is up in the loft and there are trusses of hay, too. The child makes herself nests in the straw. Tiring of this, she takes a look into the granary where there are full sacks leaning against one another and a heap of oats splaying out on the boards. Here is a pile of carrots, another of mangolds, and some linseed cake. She gives the handle of the slicing machine a turn, and another to the winch which winds the chain for pulling up sacks. Then she raises the hatch and looks down to the coach-house beneath which is empty except for the red sledge. It was a rare treat to go out in that vehicle. The harness bells tinkled as this fairy-tale carriage glided along the snowy roads. There was room for two or three passengers on

11

the front seat, and the coachman was perched on a single one behind, the reins passing overhead. But in spite of fur rugs, muffs, and a foot warmer, even the child had to admit feeling a bit cold. It was delightful by the fireside to hear about the Snow Queen in her sledge, but to imitate her way of getting about had its drawbacks.

The child returns to the main loft; she peeps down the chute for oats with a certain amount of awe, for she is small enough to fall down and get stuck. Then she sits by the open hatch overlooking the yard. It is raining, not hard, but she can see drops falling by the edge of the house roof opposite Overhead the weather-cock makes a squeaky moan. Horse noises come from the stable below, from Paul of uncertain temper and the grey stallion, The Czar. When the rain stops, a flight of pigeons from a neighbour's loft circles the house. This loft is a thrilling place to the child; she can get up here by the iron ladder flush with the wall, but getting down again is beyond her courage. Now she wants to go out into the gardens, so she calls and calls, and at length Walter's reassuring form, in shirt and waistcoat, appears in the hatch above the ladder. He leans back, takes her in his arms and puts her on the ladder. Then, one day she found she could slip on to it herself; it marked the end of an epoch in childhood.

When I went for a ride on Patrick on a pad-saddle, Walter used to walk in his waistcoat behind. We went along lanes between hedges, and the donkey walked on at a slow trot, leaving Walter behind. Then the donkey put his head down for a tuft of grass, and the saddle with it. But I was not hurt. Walter the groom had a fund of information, he knew which were bad and which were good villages. The pretty ones all seemed too 'bad' or liberal after a long period with Noel Buxton as the member of Parliament. Walter was a Tory like his master.

Bacon the coachman had been with my father and grandfather for a great number of years, for both father and son had been doctors at Holt. He was looked upon as one of the best horsemen in Norfolk. However, one day a strange vehicle came into the yard. It was a French motor car, a de Dion-Bouton. It was open with a hood for rainy weather, a single cylinder, and the top speed was 25 miles per hour. It had a 'Stepney', or spare wheel, clamped on by the driver's seat, for on the rough stony roads, punctures were common. Cars were rare and people

12

ran to their garden gates to see one pass. My father came out of the house to look at the car. He must keep up with the times, but he much preferred his thoroughbred horses, and kept two for a period.

I was much alone, but occasionally had another child to play with, and for company outside in secret, there was the gardener and the gardener's boy. In season there was plenty of fruit, which I was allowed to eat, and never seemed to upset myself. Especially I remember the white raspberry canes. I would wend my way along them picking some red fruit, and at the extreme end there were some white ones. I wonder if there are white raspberries now?

My House

Now a word about the house in which I was destined to spend 90 years. To have lived in several homes must have divided life into compartments, and a series of scenes, some wistfully remembered. A single home since the dawn of memory is all embracing. It has a spirit, almost a personality, from which there is no escape. What the place was like in the past, what one has heard about it, is as remote as history, just a tale that has been told. It is the sequence of years remembered personally, and of times so dimly recollected that they fade into a dream, which makes up the 'personality' of the home.

The child has progressed into old age, and now the place is hers, but many things about it have been changeless. Within the thick walls of the house it has been always cool in summer heat, and warm down in the cellar on a cold winter's day.

Precedence allows old faults to continue. The sky-light has dripped for as long as memory in a downpour - no bricklayer could keep it sound for more than a few months - and there are little cracks of sound as the raindrops strike the passage beneath. Scratches on doors made by long-dead dogs remain - it has never been any good erasing them, for lively dogs will make more! Bow windows added a century ago have pulled the garden front out of straight, so that sash windows do not close properly at the top - use has accustomed residents to draught.

But there has been change going on almost imperceptibly. Suddenly one is aware that plaster has all but gone from the early Victorian south

13

front, revealing mellow brick, and gradually the century-old coating of tar on the stables has faded away, showing the pebbles in natural colours - both changes for the better. But the gardener's bell under the canopy high up on the wall has gone - it was unsafe - and only the bell-pull in the beamed kitchen remains.

The yard of red and blue bricks, flag-stone and cobble, is busy no longer with the washing of carriages or motor cars; when it dries after winter rain and snow it is a patchwork of clean colour - a sign of the spring. The house itself is not aloof from neighbours - beyond the drive steep, roofs huddle over cosy yards. Pigeons cling to the tiles and there is an undertone of coo-ing. The narrow street twists on to the wide one of the market town between serene Georgian houses.

The oak at the corner of the yard looks about the same size as in a photograph more than a hundred years old. A pair of turtle doves make a purring noise within the leaves. An ancient mulberry was there, but the yew fences are missing, and a cedar deodar on the lawn, now over-topping the house, was so small that a lad could jump higher. Now the breeze in its branches makes a slight sound, as of the sea. Trees tend to be planted too close together, the planter failing to visualise ultimate growth. In the paddock, a pink chestnut, marking the

The oldest surviving photograph of the house taken prior to 1899. Jane's grandfather, John Hales, is on the extreme right

grave of a favourite horse, now almost touches another gree. And gales can shatter life-long landmarks. A cedar of lebanon was uprooted one wild morning; its flat top had been a refuge of chidhood. Beneath it was a butcher's broom, which perished, but the rockery survived, a dingy Victorian relic. In this stone-less county, large pieces of cork had been used as a substitute for rock. Overgrown with periwinkle and ferns, this dusky place had escaped the attention or daunted the spirit of any reforming gardener.

Of the same date is the summerhouse built in an angle of two old walls. Its beetling brows of ivy-root and reed thatch exclude sunbeams further than the threshold. Here, on the stone floor, are remnants of garden furniture, and the place has a distinctive smell. The thatch on the roof is covered with ivy; a patch of nettles has taken root there, and honeysuckle too.

In contrast to this rather morbid spot, is a strip of raised garden beneath the high wall facing west. Here, in full sunshine, blazes a riot of california poppies and marigold. They are self-sown, but who scattered the original seed? The lower part of the wall is of orange mouldering brick, but the top section, bearing the date 1879 is dull red. On the cold eastern side of the wall is the 'iron pear' of unknown age or correct name, and a morello cherry, flinging out its boughs of tempting but disappointing fruit. Here is the 'new' kitchen garden, taken in from the meadow nearly eighty years ago. The paths are edged with wavy bricks and perennial plants, and the place is happily haunted by the spirit of the old man who worked there as a lad and a very old man. In his young days, he helped to set the bricks by the paths, and in extreme age he straightened them out afresh. At six p.m. he was still busy. When remonstrated with, he replied, 'When I works to oblige, I works to oblige!' The 'collier dog' who could do no wrong, lay by his side. Occasionally he paused to light his pipe, which was thrust into his pocket when anybody appeared. Many are the plants which perpetuate him; every year a few straggling wallflowers bloom which he had set, and no one had the heart to pull up.   .

'That there grass, that wants cutting again.' How often has this been heard, especially in early summer, or after a dose of sulphate of ammonia on the lawn! Somehow it seems a shame to shear all that pushing exuberant growth. Walking over it one finds a pale blue starling's egg - some bird has been taken short - or just a frail broken shell. But the grass must be cut, it will not look attractive later on. This is a comparatively easy and unskilled job - but noisy - all processes seem to be getting noisier these times. More than a hundred years ago, the scythe, set well back, did the job in a trained man's hands, and it made a nice sound too, alternating with that of the edge being sharpened on a stone. Now any fool can cut the lawn.

Francis Bacon advocated a green of four acres, but then his princely garden was thirty acres in extent. 'The Green hath two pleasures: the one because nothing is more pleasant to the eye than green grass kept finely shorn.' And it all had to be with a scythe! In 1767 someone complained of lawns being so badly mown that every stroke of the scythe appears, 'they have a very disagreeable appearance'. Before mowing it was recommended to roll and pole the grass. The latter was done with a long pliable rod to remove worm casts etc. Great attention was paid to edges, and sheep shears were advised to cut them with.

To come to the present century, it used to be the 'dickey' who pulled the machine. 'Turn towards yer work,' shouted the man between the handles to his assistant leading the demure animal. So the alternate lanes of vivid green and silver-green were drawn across the smooth sward, and woe betide the workers if the lines were squiggly! It was a let down to the garden if they were not straight; on the dry light Norfolk earth there was no need for the donkey to wear leather shoes. The bane of the lawn was the daisies, not to mention plantains, which the weed-killer did not harm. Patience did it, and the owner on his knees for twenty years, with a little totty fork, freed the grass of weeds - but after he had gone they grew again.

The days of the dickey-drawn machine were numbered. Eventually some strange men appeared with a motor one, which drank petrol and oil mixed together, and the donkey retired to the pightle, with a red cotton mask over his head to keep off the flies. After all, he would start after some prodding, but the new motor machine often refused to, and required the attentions of a mechanic to make it go. War came, and there was no petrol for the machine, so it had to be put away in the summerhouse, and the small push variety taken out. This required one puller on a cord, and one between the handles. It was slow work, but there were excitements. From the sky they started dropping silvery strands of paper-like twists - some subtle plan to defeat somebody. This fairy-like stuff was caught in the grass, but there were worse things. Once the puller stopped abruptly for an unexploded cannon shell was sticking up amongst the greenery.

When the six-year war was over, the green was a sorry sight, for half of it had been left wild. There was nothing for it but to cut with shears, upon hands and knees, and to go on doing it for months. But at last it was done; the motor mower, now old and decrepit, and even more obstinate to start, came out of retirement.

With advancing age and less free time, came the new machine with a seat. It was an ugly awe-inspiring vehicle, squat and very heavy. It made an even more hideous noise than its predecessor, and would roll and mow anything, even rough grass. Mounted on the seat there was a sense of exhilaration, and the steering stick in front might have been that of an aeroplane. Yet in spite of the infernal din, the swallows did not seem to mind, and skimmed over the green, almost touching the machine. Turning difficulties made it hard to weave the traditional pattern of straight paths across the lawn, but the work got done fast - on dry grass. In damp weather it was not so good; the chute connecting with the sack behind got choked with wet weed, and the machine did not function properly. The last cut in November was a very poor show, and the machine vomited heaps of depressing-looking stuff on the lawn. The swallows had all gone, the wind was no longer balmy, and the hands on the steering-stick were numb with cold. It was done at last, and this latest in machines was pushed back into the summerhouse for winter rest, along with old croquet hoops, some bowls jacks, and a worn-out archery target.

It is more difficult to find out how a garden has developed than the house to which it belongs. Only mellow walls, bright in the sunshine, and the persistent survival of a few outmoded flowers, suggest the antiquity of the garden. Long forgotten gardeners are now perpetuated by plants springing up each year. Some are now classed as mere weeds, as the orange hawkweed (hieracium). In the shrubbery are a few stems of monks-hood (aconitum napellus), poisonous in all its parts. Clumps of yellow corydalis spring up on old walls. No one knows when seed was first sown, perhaps two centuries ago.

Then there are the old roses which had been relegated to the kitchen garden. 'My mother's roses are all put out,' a former owner would explain regretfully. Now, many are reinstated in the 'pleasure garden'. There are the deep pink golden centred rosa gallica (origin unknown), the striped petals of rosa mundi, and a small deep red rose of wonderful scent, and unknown name. The two former bloom in lavish splendour. Growing on their own stock, they spread rapidly and are unlikely to be exterminated. By the entrance to the house was a miserable bush that had not flowered for many years. With attention, it has taken on a new life; frail and pale pink petals unfold, bringing back childhood's memories. The flowers last but a day in the sunshine, for the glory of the rose was far shorter in the past.

In the 'eighties of the last century, two little roses were put into the market - Cecille Brunner and Perle d'Or. They are still to be found in the garden. Sweet-smelling and shell-pink, they make ideal button-holes. Relegated to a distant border, out-of-fashion hybrid tea roses bloom in Edwardian magnificence, excelling many modern varieties. Dorothy Perkins is scattered about the garden, rambler of the first part of the century, and no longer popular.

The kitchen garden has altered these latter years since the old man died in the spring after he had 'mocked in' the peas. Then, a period of neglect turned much of the land into a wilderness of weed and gay seedling lupins. The potting shed has got rickety, but the 'iron pear' on the high west wall still bears fruit. A few perennials in edging borders have lasted a lifetime, and old roses, banished there at the coming of hybrid teas, show frail petals once a summer and send scent abroad. The beehives have gone from a far corner, but the crown artichokes and fennel which were near them are still there. The spirit of the place is demanding, compelling one to hoe paths which have long since lost their gravel and are seldom seen.

But sometimes history compels notice. Taking up flagstones near the house wall for new plumbing revealed an ancient well of narrow bricks, almost filled up with rubble. When the range was removed from the kitchen there was a low hearth behind it. Here, maybe, Mr Justice Jewell's dinner was cooked, and perhaps he built the kitchen wing. In

18

the nave of the parish church is a stone - 'To the memory of Edmund Jewell Esq one of his Majesty's Justices of the Peace which he executed with strict Honor. He departed this Life the 10th of November, 1784, aged 65'.

When wallpaper is removed, blocked-in doors come to light in odd places; near one of them an unaccountable sound is heard at times. There is a window alcove which now backs upon a passage, for once the building must have been slimmer.

Some time after Jewell's occupation, the house was divided into two, but it was united again when the Rev John Custance Leake came to live here in 1805. He was the rector of Beckham and Barningham Parva, for non-resident incumbents were not unusual.

In 1833 the house passed to Thomas Norris Aufrere, who belonged to a family which had fled from France after the Revocation of the Edict of Nantes. Later it was bought by a builder, John Joseph Darken, who had extravagant ideas. He added an extension to the south, and altered the structure of the house, creating two big rooms on the upper and lower storeys. It was he, no doubt, who put in the high entrance hall with the elegant staircase which he had removed, probably, from another building. All this may have helped to ruin Darken, for he went bankrupt.

Holt was burned down in 1708, but my property escaped as it was too far away. It had a big lawn at the front of the house and a depressed part, with flowers to represent heavenly bodies. The sun in the centre had rays, but cutting the edges made them misshaped and they were filled in. There were three moon-shaped beds and a planet; this had beautiful pansies in once, but they got a disease and all died in a night, so we filled in the bed. In the centre bed there were wallflowers in the spring and many coloured verbenas in the summer. Beyond the lawn was a field where Patrick the donkey grazed and had his shed. There was a summer house which had been attached, but it got covered with ivy and blew down this year.

Mr Sidney Cozens-Hardy had the deeds of the house, which he kindly copied out for me. The first owner was Robert Roper, who was succeeded in 1657 by his nephew. However, the Surveyor who came to assess the War damage thought it was probably Elizabethan, a narrow house facing west. The walls of the greater part are about 15 inches thick compared to about 9 inches now. The first person of any social status was Edmund Jewell who was in possession from 1742 to 1798. He has a memorial in Holt Church, and was a JP. He may have added the kitchen wing at right angles to the house. There were five reverend gentlemen who lived outside their parishes, just going there on a Sunday. They were the Rectors of Saxthorpe, Beckham, Barningham Parva, Stody and Hunworth, not forgetting the Rev Josiah Flavell who was Rector for 47 years and died in 1840.

John Hales, MRCS came to Holt in 1846. His father was a solicitor of Hales Court, St Giles Street, Norwich. He had considered getting a practice at Mattishall, but landed up at Holt. He married a girl from Baconsthorpe and had two sons. I have an old photograph of the house taken in 1866. John is sitting by a rustic table; he seems to have grown stout in 20 years. Two men are manipulating a small machine and his two sons are posed nearby. My grandfather built the wall along the garden and field in 1868-9, which is still standing, and reaches to the Thornage turning, also another for fruit by the kitchen garden; and also something in which he was not going to be well-served, bows over the window which pulled the house slightly out of place. I always have a draught in my bedroom. After an interval, the house passed to my own family. Indeed, it must have altered much since Robert Roper lived here during the Commonwealth.

'Put it on the cellar steps' was often the instruction about a jug of milk in the summers of the past. There was no bottle milk then; the milkman ladled it, unhygenically, out of his can into the household jug. Other foods, which wanted keeping cool, were placed in the ice-box at the bottom of the cellar. Not that this heavy old receptacle had any ice in it, but it was wonderfully cold inside. No self-respecting house, even if small, was without a cellar. Now it is shut up and neglected. Noxious things may be down there - spiders, black beetles, even rats - anyway there is dust, so the door is kept shut. The present housewife has a refrigerator handy, and the worn cellar steps are never trodden upon. At the bottom are two wine cellars with doors, some empty glass bottles, and small stone ones too, which once contained home made ginger beer. In another space, with a faint diffusion of daylight, is the ice-box, a stand for a cider cask, and a great Aladdin's jar for putting down eggs in lime. In an alcove are shelves for storing apples.

It is a different world down here, so cool in summer, and warmer than the house above on a cold winter's day. A wine cellar has a double door and a curious lock, and only the master (fortunately) could turn the key. An Aberdeen terrier followed him inside, and was shut up by mistake. It was some time before he was discovered. Then the days of peace and plenty receded, and the cellar was supposed to be the safest place in an air-raid. Camp-stools were put down there and a supply of candles, but nobody ever used them.

Nowadays a cellar can be made an attractive place. Electric light reveals the nooks and crannies, and the darkest recesses are indecently plain for the first time in history. One, with a fine brick arched roof, has been whitewashed, and used for a store for antiques; in alcoves are flowered china plates instead of bottles. Another has slots cut in the stone steps, and a ring attached to the top stair. Two poles were put in these slots, and casks, roped to the ring, were lowered carefully into the cellar. The main beam supporting the place is about one foot thick. Much smuggled stuff found its way into cellars, and Parson Woodforde saw no harm in 'bottling Moonshine'.

Attics can be packed with memories as well as junk, memories so old that they merge into dreams. From the dormer windows one has looked out on never-to-be-forgotten events, and the past is a series of views from their aloof heights. The attics of which I write are very old, with rough-hewn floorboards from some ancient saw pit. Far away over the Norfolk countryside they look, to distant churches and plantations, Trees have grown up beneath them and over-topped the house, cottages have been pulled down beneath, new roadways made.

Louisa lay ill abed in the Cook's attic. When she was about, most of her day from breakfast onwards was occupied in getting the dinner. Now she had nothing to do but listen to the water gurgling in the new water tanks. The noise gave her the creeps and she could not abide it, so a young woman from over the way came to bear her company, and reassure her against the mysterious modern noises. Now and again a small child was sent up from the depths of the house, bringing her some delicacy from the distant kitchen. When Louisa was well she used to read aloud from a book of fairy stories, but ever afterwards the events of the Snow Queen seemed to be chasing through these attics.

Outside the window was the starry sky; it was eerie inside by candlelight. The child held fast to a reassuring hand. There it was, the Comet, not Halley's which should have arrived, but another one which had come unexpectedly - the child rather wished it hadn't, for she was a bit afraid of it. The aurora borealis she was equally in awe of, for had it not something to do with the roaring bull of Farmer Ellis, up the road?

Then there was the Far Attic, the low door of which was opened by a curious key, quite distinct from the others on the household bunch. Here were odds and ends, the boxes of Christmas Tree ornaments which were brought downstairs on an exciting day in December, a Noah's Ark trunk filled with copies of the *Illustrated London News* from the times of the Boer War, and the Jubilees, and lengths of soap laid out on slats to dry. It was Maria's job to fetch a supply in a fish basket. Quite pleased with herself was the old woman as she climbed the steep stair, talking to the dog at her heels, for fetching the soap she considered a privilege. On the attic window sill was an ornate glass candlestick hung about with pendants. It was a broken piece of finery but, acting as a prism, it threw splashes upon the boards.

From the tall pole in the field, the lines of the first wireless aerial entered an attic window. What a complicated affair it was, with instruments strewn all over the table! To the eager listeners came the time signal from the Eiffel Tower in Morse Code. Before they had learnt to decipher the dots and dashes efficiently the Great War broke out; the apparatus was taken off to the police station, and the boy who had assembled it joined the Army.

The second war came. One summer night I was woken by a tremendous bang. A terrific explosion shook the old house; glass tinkled from the windows. The sleeping town woke in an instant. My bed was across the window and I could see smoke rising from a field about half a mile to the south. I put on my siren suit and ran the length of the house to the attic stairs to get a better look and then went up to the town where I met the Wardens in a bunch. I told them where the bomb had fallen.

Dust was tinkling from the windows on to the sleepers, but no-one was hurt. The next day I moved my bed to between the windows for protection. The Wardens had found the big shallow crater of a land mine and another had fallen on the other side of Holt near an empty house. The next day I got a reprimand for not reporting the name of a lady whose nose had bled. [See also p.60]

During the war years the attics were swept and bare. Nobody dreamt there any more of a sweetheart. Then V-Day came at last, and the dwellers in the house watched the fireworks on the Common from the attic windows.

The old house was being altered - separated into four parts, and the builders were making a hole in the floor of the Far Attic to communicate with Part One. Then a ladder was put up on the landing beneath, and an astonished head poked through the opening. For that attic had been the very end of the world, separated from the landing by a long passage and stairs, by many steps. Now it could be reached in a few seconds; it was quite uncanny.

For months the newly-garnished attics were desolate. The darkened casements rattled in the cold, windy nights, the sleeping butterfly in a crevice was the only life within. Then one night the home-bound traveller at the gate looked up at the house and behold, there was light pouring out of an attic window - electric light for the first time in history.

There was a small field beyond the lawn, an ancient mulberry tree propped up, and a walnut. John had the adjoining 7 acres of field for hay and his horses. Robert had a tennis court made on the little field. How it was levelled I should like to know.

Rodbaston

Come now to my own memories of Rodbaston where I spent weeks on end at one time. It was a day's journey to get there by the old Midland and Great Northern Railway, and as I was a bad traveller I was often sick.

We went westward across the fens to Melton Mowbray and on to Leicester. Here we went into a restaurant and had pea soup. At Birmingham I was taken to the Pet Market, and coveted in vain nearly every puppy, rabbit and guinea pig. Onwards in the dusk through the glow of the Black Country to Wolverhampton station, where we went to see an ex-housemaid from Rodbaston who kept a waiting room; then through the fields to Gailey station and up the steep slope to the waiting carriage. I can still hear the sound of the horses.

Out of the darkness into the light and warmth of the hall with its a big stove, organ, and fine spiral staircase up to the top storey. Here was the nursery and Lucy Dawkins waiting there to hug me. She was Granny's maid and a 'Mrs' with some sad story behind her which I never heard. Tea was on the table. Lucy went to a corner cupboard for something, it had a spicy smell, and she knocked on the floor with a stick to tell Granny's nurse that tea was ready. There were pikelets which I only tasted in Staffordshire. When the tea cups were empty the message of the tea leaves caused much merriment.

Afterwards I went to bed, for children were sent early then. I shared with my mother the 'canopy' room on a lower storey and slept in a little bed near hers. There was a fire in the grate. On one occasion I took with me a small electric torch. Two housemaids came in to turn down the big bed and were horrified at what they took for a flame beneath my sheet; they had never seen electric light. When I woke in the morning there was some fruit on a plate near my bed which mother had brought up from dessert. Soon, the early morning tea tray arrived. Breakfast for me was in the nursery; porridge, and bacon and eggs. Mother told me that in her young days she had only bread and milk.

The nursery had two windows, one looking out on the park and away to Cannock Chase, and the other to distant Wrekin. Here Polly Everall sat who came to do the household mending. She could look out

Rodbaston

of the house and see the sugar loaf hill of the rock rising in Shropshire. From the other window, away over the Park was the dark line of Cannock Chase. Conspicuous in the room was the rocking horse. It had a hole in one side and its tummy rattled and gurgled as it rocked to and fro. Pencils and other objects which had been dropped down by mistake could never be retrieved. I added to them a silver pencil my uncle Leonard had given me, and that made me sad when I failed to retrieve it as others had before me.

After breakfast I was sent to say 'Good morning' to my Granny. She was always sitting in a straight-backed chair by her bed, a big woman dressed in black with a white widow's cap, and she would be humming continually a low tune. Once she called me to her to do up my dress. 'Hump', she said, 'Your mother ought to dress you in Nun's veiling'. When I repeated this to my mother she was quite indignant. I faintly remember seeing Granny downstairs in a cane chair. She must have been brought there in the lift near her bedroom. It was worked by ropes which the footmen pulled and was the first type of lift which I ever saw. I don't think my grandmother was a happy woman. Racked with pain she could no longer play the organ in the hall - she had been a good musician. Also, she was by nature a very generous person, longing to

25

give presents. In this she was partially prevented by her eldest son, Herbert, when he visited her, for he had an estate of his own not far away, but then, as now, money bred trouble!

When I was very young I used to be taken for a morning walk by Elsie Myatt who was in her teens and the butler's daughter. Her family lived at the Lodge at the end of the drive. First we went to the rockery on one side of the garden pool. It was a typical Victorian one, gloomy with ferns. Here I came face to face with a peacock and was told it was an 'enchanter' and might turn me into a toad. I only half believed this, but it gave me a lifelong fascination with these birds. After that we went through to the road and came to the farm buildings, the gloom of the cow and bullock stalls. Here were peafowl again, perched on rafters, splashes of colour. I longed to ascend the central water tower which supplied the estate, but was not allowed to. At the first Jubilee of 1887, one of my uncles, who may have had a drop too much, went up to put a flag on top, and slipped into the water tank and got a drenching.

Mrs Potham at Rodbaston Farm

Beyond the buildings was a gas-holder put there by Shaw-Helier to supply the estate. Further on, on the opposite side of the road, there was a fine old farmhouse which some Philistine has now demolished. It ought to have been a listed building. Here we were greeted by Mrs Potham and taken down to the dairy where there were wide pans of milk topped with cream. Mrs Potham would fill a small glass of cream with a skimmer and give it to me to drink. It was delicious. I had tasted milk fresh from the cow, which was tepid, and I did not like it. In those far-off days there was no artificial separation. On a shelf were butter moulds, ranging from various models of a swan, to an acorn. Mrs Potham said the swan was only used on cricket weeks.

When I grew older, I spent much time in a small boat on the water in the garden where there was no risk of drowning as the water was very shallow. I went to the walled kitched garden outside which was the 'bothy', the home of two bachelor gardeners. I went into the greenhouse. Inside was a muscat vine. The grapes were so delicious they spoiled my taste for other varieties. Then there was the banana tree in a very hot house. From it hung the 'hands' of green fruit, some ripening to yellow, and we took some home with us.

There was fishing as another pastime. Nobody could make me put a worm on a hook so I resorted to dough. I tried my luck in the garden pool in my own special stance which was down a steep narrow track to a level patch of ground. One day whilst I was fishing I heard Lucy Dawkins calling me urgently. Aeroplanes were expected to pass over in a race. We went on to the road near the farm buildings. Sure enough, an aeroplane appeared and flew over the buildings, but not as high as the tower. I was thrilled. It was the first 'plane' I had seen, and it must have been a very primitive type. That evening Aunt Margie went to a dinner at Stafford and sat next to one of the pilots. He said to her 'We shall be killed in these machines'. He was, soon after. Those men were the pioneers of the modern jets of today, which carry millions in safety.

One morning Mrs Myatt, the housekeeper-cum-cook, beckoned me into her sanctum and gave me a cigarette card depicting some potentate seated in a kind of boat and flying through the air drawn by a flock of big birds. This intrigued me, and I wondered why it had not been tried. I longed to fly, but it was many years before my wish was gratified.

About a mile from Rodbaston were the three Gailey Pools, which were reservoirs which had been rented by the Wards since they were made. Often I spent a day there with Elsie. We went across the park, the noisy rookery, to the lock in the canal. When a barge went through I looked with awe into the depths. A barge was drawn along by a horse on the tow path. It was a short distance from here to the Big Pool, and on reaching the edge we called loudly to Haynes, the keeper, to bring a boat and row us - which he would do if he felt like it. Otherwise we had to walk round quite a long way. The water was clear and pure and dragonflies gave colour amongst the reeds. When we arrived at the boat house we would see the heavy Welsh fishing boats. By this time we would be hungry, and so would go into the house to eat our sandwiches. The boats were too heavy for a child to row, and I got jeered when I failed to keep one still with the oars for my elders who were fishing. Sometimes I was allowed to fish in the bait trap but even there was not successful.

In the park, hay was being cut and I had a small rake. It had splinters in it which ran into my fingers. My nose ran, through mild hay fever. Nevertheless it was fun playing hide and seek with the others amongst the haycrops.

In the summer when the water was warm enough, mother and I went to bathe at the other end of the pool where there was a soft mossy bottom for the feet. Mother wore a blue costume from neck to pantaloons, a skirt over it and frilled sleeves to below the shoulders. What a contrast to the bikini of today!

There was an island in the middle of the Big Pool and one springtime a heron nested in a tree there. Contrary to modern thought I was allowed a collection of different eggs and longed for a heron's. A lad came and said he would get one for me. He rowed to the island and began to climb the tree but, as it happened, a carrion crow was nesting in another tree. This bird flew at the lad so ferociously that he had to descend in a hurry. I did not get a heron's egg.

One autumn when I was at Rodbaston, my uncle had a shooting party. I was with one of the guns in a small plantation in the park, and frightened rabbits were taking refuge there. I pleaded with my companion not to shoot, and to his great credit he refrained.

28

We had several excursions from Rodbaston. Lucy Dawkins, my sister, and Nickerson went in the new Ford car to the sugar-loaf hill of the Wrekin, in Shropshire. I looked through the 'eye of a needle' (two rocks) and saw the Stiperstones gleaming in the distance. Aunt Margie took my sister and I to the cinema at Stafford. Of course it was a silent film, but I had never seen one before.

Grandmother in her donkey-drawn carriage

My grandmother died in the spring of 1914. Mother was there at the time and I joined her afterwards. There was an air of depression about the place; the worst of it was when I awoke with a fever. Granny's nurse who was still there came to me and said 'You should not worry your mother like this'. I did not know how I could help it. Next day I was better.

Nobody knew what was going to happen as the heir, my uncle George, lived in the United States. In August the Great War broke out. Mother said it was a mercy Granny had not lived to see it, for she would have grieved so if the horses had been commandeered. During the war the house was left with a skeleton staff. Uncle George came over in 1919 and mother and I made a short stay there. His intention was to sell Rodbaston and buy a smaller house in England, but his wife, an American, persuaded him to go back. The pull of a large family got him back to the States in the end. Some of his boys and girls had stayed at Rodbaston and had been laughed at for calling jerseys 'pull-overs' as the word had not been introduced into England at that time. Eventually, when it was sold for an Agricultural College, my mother was quite pleased as she loved nature and was a very keen gardener

I think, in its heyday, Rodbaston had been a happy community. It was largely self-supporting; even letters had to be fetched by a groom from Penkridge. There was a big enough household staff (nine) for nobody to be overworked, and food and accommodation were good. Years afterwards one of them said to me, 'Oh, for the happy days at Rodbaston'.

In the nursery were rows of *Little Folks*, a famous children's book. I was told I could have six. They were beautifully clean and in perfect condition. I still have them for sentiment's sake, although I think that they have grown quite valuable. Far better was Taffy, the Welsh pony which had pulled the chair. I rode him frequently about the Norfolk countryside, all alone.

Frances and Jane at the time of their visits to Rodbaston

The Oddy's Woods

As a child I was fascinated by the stories of Mrs Molesworth, that classic writer for the young, and there was a real Christmas Tree Land visible from my bedroom window. Away, over the field and hedges was an edge of dark wood, one tree high above the others, a big tree I could never find in the wood itself. Old Mr Oddy, the owner and architect of this unusual wood, had been a wool merchant in Leeds, and had retired to Norfolk.

On winter mornings a rosy ball moved up from the dark horizon. From this small forest came the household Christmas tree, chosen in exciting minutes with Mr Oddy and carried home in the donkey-drawn 'tumble'. He gave his white house corner pinnacles, and set a couple of heraldic beasts on the gate pillars at the drive's entrance. In spite of what the critical might have said about the interior of the house, it was enthralling to the child. Beams had been carved by Mr Oddy himself, who had a passion for wood, and on one of them I spelt out 'East, West, Home's Best'. This was a pleasant house facing south, with a view over lawn and ha-ha to the long rough meadows sheltered by trees from the east wind.

His wife did not like company. When the parlour maid opened the door, only her back could be seen going up the stairs. Mr Oddy had no sporting interests, so he engaged a local poacher to keep out the others, and reward himself from wild life as he chose. Tenth (so called because he was the youngest of ten sons) was a small man who walked with head down and gun under his arm, greeting a few by a touch of the cap. One old man was allowed to pass unmolested through Tenth's domain because he claimed to be treading an ancient right-of-way which crossed the heath before the trees sprang up.

There was a brick archway, to the wilder wood. Beyond was bell heather, and further on the dark firs closed in to a junction of paths with a statue in the middle. There were other paths and statues; one of the latter had lost a breast, which injury a decorous Victorian had concealed with a bandage from shoulder to waist.

The woods ended at a common, where owners and occupiers of ancient houses had the privilege of cutting peat and grazing one head of stock. Just within his boundary was a wooden look-out from which Mr Oddy and his friends could admire the rolling view of heath and fields.

In a wartime summer, a yeomanry regiment from the Shires camped on rough meadow; a spurred trumpeter with a bandolier blew the afternoon call to water horses, and the sound carried into the woods to my ears.

To me the place was a frequent playground, from autumn when scarlet toadstools appeared amid the close trunks of the pines, to winter when Barker's Pit, a pool in the woods, was frozen and I tried to skate on an old pair of wooden skates with metal blades. In spring there was birds' nesting, and once I espied two sleeping owls on a lower branch of a giant pine; the thrill of that experience I never forgot. Late summer brought swarms of flies on the picnic spread. In the woods I learnt to balance on my bicycle and ride silently along the paths in an ecstasy of speed.

After old Mr Oddy died, his family continued living in the pinnacled white house; his widow, a small silent woman, and his son Douglas, quiet as his mother, who often went into the wood with me and my elder sister, who was already of age. The company of Douglas was an asset to my enjoyment of Christmas Tree Land. Barker's Pit had an old boat-house, but the boat had degenerated into a few rotten boards, so Douglas made a raft out of a door and petrol cans. The pool was shallow, fed with springs, and the raft supported one person at a time satisfactorily, but when the three of us got on, it sank beneath our weight. The water pulled off my skirt and petticoat. 'I think you have lost something', said Douglas, shyly.

At the edge of the woods was a bog called the Lows and on Sundays and holidays, townspeople used to walk around the Lows, but now so many have cars they go further afield. The Lows have been designated as having a natural and scientific importance because of this bog, where there are rare mosses and sundew flowers, whose leaves catch and devour insects.

The child is a materialist, longing for treasure, treasure that can be admired and handled, and the obvious source in that country place was the bird's nest. Till the eye became trained, the search was difficult, and the find hedged around with prohibitions; one egg might be taken if there were four in the nest, and a wren's must be extracted with a spoon or the bird would forsake. Never-to-be-forgotten were the nightjar's eggs, so beautifully marked with brown and purple, lying on a bare patch amongst the heather; the bird itself was so strange - put you in mind of a cat.

Butterflies were more treasure, condemned by the heartless to the killing-bottle, and pinned out in a wooden case. How beautiful they were, from the pale blue ones to the gay peacocks and red admirals! Always there was the hope of catching a great swallow-tail.

Douglas stretched a platform of rabbit netting up between some tall trees. The ascent was made by means of a rope, and notches in a trunk. But one day I lost Douglas and my sister. I called and called but there was no response. At last I found them beyond the trees in a more open place of brambles, sweet briar and short turf. I was a bit surprised that they had left me but thought little of it. Soon after this I went away to a boarding school and one day received a letter which gave me quite a shock. Douglas and my sister were engaged to be married. My parents were not altogether pleased with the match as Douglas was so much older than she, and he was only one amongst many other admirers.

Frances' wedding, 10 June, 1920, in the garden at Holt

During the 1939-45 war, the wood was felled and later replanted with rows of pine, an economic undertaking. The old paths have disappeared, and broken statues are covered with undergrowth. The red archway stands there in a different aspect. Newcomers, who know nothing of Christmas Tree Land, stare at it and wonder why it was built. But near Barker's Pit stands an old Scotch pine with ruddy branches. The sight of it brings together present and past for some folk.

Kings Hills

About 3/4 of a mile from my home in Holt along the Hunworth road was a track across a meadow leading to a grassy ridge with a few big trees and a valley with dark dense conifers right to the skyline. There was brown bracken, and we used to go there with Taffy and the 'tumble' and go and cut the bracken for the pony's loose box. The bracken was cut with a sickle. Occasionally I would get up early, before breakfast, and take Taffy there to admire the view. Why was it called King's Hills? My Father said it was because it belonged to someone called King. Both my sister and I enjoyed going there.

Francis Craven

He was the son of Mr and Mrs Craven who lived at Heath House before my sister married. Francis was a little older than myself. His hobby was running toy trains around a track he had made at the edge of the wood. I liked playing at conjuring myself, and that was more of an indoor pursuit.

The Cravens had a two-seater motor car. Mrs Craven was a smart little woman who used to be driven by her husband; she would make polite little bows to all her acquaintances. Francis wanted to join the Royal Navy and was interviewed by a high-ranking Officer. He was then sent to Osborn College on the Isle of Wight. He was in a dormitory with about 20 other boys. When they were called in the mornings they had to get up at once and run and jump into a small swimming bath full of cold water. Just before the end of the course when he jumped in, he found the bath was empty. Years afterwards my brother Bobby, who was an Officer in the Royal Navy, met Francis Craven, and told him he had noticed his servant was packing his belongings. When asked why he was doing this, the servant said he did not know why, only that he was to go ashore. Bobby thought he might have had a mental breakdown. That was the last we heard of Francis Craven.

Blakeney Point

I ought to have mentioned Blakeney Point before the Oddy's woods for it was my paradise. It ran out from Cley in a north-westerly direction parallel to the shore and was shingle and sand hills. Professor Oliver was surveying it and there were several boats and huts, boats like Noah's Ark. We stayed in a hut belonging to the Rector of Cley for several nights.

In the pit of the channel opposite were some old oyster boats and we fished from them and only caught useless little crabs. I wandered on the sand hills, and found many skylarks with brown eggs in their nests. There was no water on the Point, and it all had to be brought from Morston. One night there was a terrible tempest and I was terrified. It was said the rocket apparatus saved us from being struck by lightning.

The next year my brother and sister were lent a barge called the *Yankee* but I was only allowed to go for the day. The first thing I did on coming aboard was to go to the cabin, throw myself on my knees and pray to stay the night, but my prayer was not answered.

Before Armageddon

The year before Europe was torn apart by the first Armageddon, my brother, Bobby, kept a diary for about six months. Now, none but the elderly remember the subjects of his jottings, though a younger generation will have read about them in history books.

On January 2nd 1913 he wrote, 'Began to paint my pole which is to be used for wireless, it does not seem to be in very sound condition'. Nevertheless the tall pole was erected in the 'pightle' about 50 yards from the house. The line from it came indoors through an attic window and down to the schoolroom where the apparatus filled a table, all of which could now be condensed into a few inches. Strange to say, it worked! Through earphones the listener could hear the time signal from the Eiffel Tower in Paris in Morse Code; the time of the spoken voice was still far in the future.

When Bobby came home for the Easter holidays he betook himself one afternoon with Walter the groom, myself as a small child, and the donkey in the shafts of the 'tumble' (tumbril) to a lime kiln about a mile away. They were met by 'Dicker Hell', so called from the way he was supposed to treat his donkey. He was white from cap to boots and he provided the lime for preserving eggs when the price fell to roughly tenpence a score. When Dicker Hell died his successor's lime was no good for the purpose.

After getting a sack of lime we went, for my benefit, birds-nesting in the shrubby slopes of the pit but all that was found was a blue hedge sparrow's egg which I picked and Bobby 'put it in my pocket where it broke'.

Bobby had left school and been sent to a 'crammer' at Clifton. He had an important exam ahead but the result was delayed. He wrote home, 'These marks would have got me into Sandhurst' but they were not high enough for entry to the Royal Military Academy at Woolwich, for he wanted to be a Sapper or Gunner.

Bobby had a run of bad luck. The weather was depressing. 'Rain again this afternoon prevented my doing anything.' His landlady gave him a poor dinner. 'Some doubtful looking meat floating in a sea of grease dotted with islands of carrots. Made a row about it.' To cap it all he put a sovereign into a slot machine in mistake for a halfpenny. 'I wrote to the owners of the machine at Bristol today, I suppose I shall get it back.'

Home never seems to have been far from Bobby's thoughts for he was an affectionate lad and concerned when his mother and sister had bad attacks of measles. 'Received a letter from Mother today who says she is better, the letter was so highly perfumed with carbolic acid that a horse outside has contracted poisoning and has since died!' On a Sunday Bobby was lonely. 'No book to read, wrote an essay on the value of good humour. The German band went on playing till 8.30 this evening. I should think they must make something of it to play like that all day.'

He had interests besides his own ambitions. On February 11th he had written 'Great sensations in the papers; death of Capt. Scott and his party, apparently more than a year ago.' Later, 'Home Rule Bill rejected by the Lords after three days debate.' On April 23rd, 'Scutari fell early this morning or late last night. Daily Telegraph vomits usual Austrophile rot. Pall Mall Gazette is very sensible.' Balkan states had attacked Turkey in an attempt to wrest from the Turks their European provinces. The Balkan League was largely successful, Russia backing it, hoping to get a hold on the Turkish states in the Mediterranean. On the other side, Austria was antagonistic fearing Serbian territory. Ambassadors met in London to try and settle the dispute, fearful of the engagement of the great powers.

Bobby went to the pictures to see the Derby. 'Could not see much of the Suffragette accident, it was over so quickly.' A Mrs Davison had run out on to the course, grasped the reins of the King's horse and brought it down. She died later of her injuries. 'Mrs Pankhurst was taken back to Holloway Prison. I should think she will die this time.' (She didn't).

Bobby often went to museums and for lonely bike rides. 'Went out biking beyond Westfield. I picked a large bunch of cowslips. The weather has been perfectly lovely today. I stayed reading on the Downs till 6.30. A friend had a new electric lamp for a bicycle, it had a small dynamo operated by the front wheel.'

On July 2nd Bobby went to London for his exams. 'Had to take taxi to King's College, Strand, arriving only just in time. Had practical chemistry and physics'. After two days he returned to Norfolk to await his fate, and the diary ends on the 19th July. Further memories reveal that Bobby passed his exam and entered the Royal Military Academy at Woolwich. The next year he was commissioned into the Garrison Artillery. He survived the carnage in Belgium and France with a wound. Later he served in campaigns in the Middle East, transferred to a mountain battery with the guns drawn by mules.

The First War begins

One day I was walking with my Auntie Carrie when we met Douglas
Oddy. He got off his bicycle and said 'Russia is mobilizing, we shall be
at war'. We called Aunt Carrie the Nun because she was dressed like
one, but she was really a Sister of Mercy.

That night I was awakened from sleep by the dogs barking and we
were told war had been declared against Austria and Germany and that
mother had gone out to see if the Territorials had all they wanted as
they had been called up. A few days later a battalion of the London
Cyclists arrived in Holt and some went on to Weybourne as there was
deep water there and invasion was possible. My father was their MO.
It was four miles to Weybourne and I went in the army lorry with him.

A few weeks after, my sister was sent with me to an aunt in
Staffordshire for safety - I did not like this and was glad when I got
home after three weeks.

One day mother told me to take a message to a widow; 'Say our
number is Norfolk 98, she will know what it means'. Mother had been
asked to be Commandant of a Voluntary Aid Detachment. Mr Sidney
Cozens-Hardy had lent his house at Letheringsett, a mile from Holt, as
a convalescent hospital for soldiers from the war hospital at Norwich,
many of them suffering from shell shock. They had a fully-trained nurse
as matron and the use of voluntary helpers from the neighbourhood.
My mother went to the hospital, and sometimes I went as well and gave
out Woodbine cigarettes to the patients, who wore blue suits, white
shirts and red ties.

After a time the German zeppelins made raids and dropped some
bombs on East Dereham, and several people were killed. The German
Command said they had hit Norwich. I am sure I saw a zeppelin. It
woke me during the night, but nobody believed me!

When I was about 12 I used to go out with some other girls to play
hockey at Home Place. It was a 'cram' for boys for the universities or
professions, and for officers in the Forces. They wore pink shirts. One
of them was called Henry. After he had left he became a pilot in the
Flying Corps, which later became the RAF. One morning Henry landed
his plane on the hockey field. He got my father to take a telegram to his

base, 'Sorry, engine trouble'. My father laughed and said 'not stomach trouble?' He was staying for lunch at Home Place.

One day I was standing in the back drive and saw such a funny looking balloon in the sky. It was boat-shaped, with people in it, flags flying and ropes hanging down. I was told it was to do with the Coastguards.

School Days

In the 1914-18 war, Britain ran the risk of starvation till Lloyd George introduced the convoy system against the German U-boats. However, the shortage of supplies restricted menus. In our house, baking of bread was done at home and a percentage of potato was used to supplement the flour. Margarine was not nearly as good as now, and it was sometimes mixed with butter.

My mother suspected I should not be fed properly at school, and she was probably right. I had two friends who went to Boarding School, who reported how hungry they were. Mother had never been to school, but went to some ladies in London, one of whom had been one of Lewis Carroll's "Three Alices", to finish her education.

I went to school when I was 15, passing through London for the first time. The school was called Highfield, near Pinner in Hertfordshire, and held 60 girls. We were ushered into the drawing room. The Headmistress, Miss Wallis, looked as if she had been moulded into her clothes and had good features and personality. Her sister Miss Laura had a pink complexion and fair hair somewhat astray. She was a music teacher and was devoted to her garden. Miss Wallis said to my mother, 'What is your daughter's name?' and my mother said 'We call her Jenny or Jane, but her proper name is Jane'. Miss Wallis replied, 'Jane is a good name, Jane it shall be. Now you shall look round the school'. She opened the door and said to the girl waiting there, 'This is a new girl, Jane Hales, will you show her round'. After all these years I forget her Christian name, but remember that her surname was Green. 'Look at all these beautiful pillars', she said. I was not impressed, but said nothing. The house was reminiscent of a French château. The school had moved there some few years earlier, from Hendon, before getting swamped by London.

For the first few days I was simply dazed. I could not do any gym, because I had no tunic and had to watch. When my tunic did arrive, it was far too big and of thick stuff, not at all smart.

The school was divided into studies. The Upper, of about seven or eight girls, was at the top, with sundry privileges, like having tea on your own and being able to gorge on birthday cakes; the West, was the biggest, the Library came next and the Junior was the smallest. I was in the Library and shared a shelf with Winifred de Mowbray, who was very queer and pinched my pens and pencils, so that I got into trouble in class. From other signs she must have been mentally deficient and had disappeared the following term.

I slept in a dormitory of six, in the bed by the door. Irene was the head. No books were allowed up there, but when I showed Irene my precious *John's Book of Birds* she said it would be all right to keep it in my drawer. We each had a china wash basin, jug and pail to empty it in and got a bath about three times a week. Miss Bradshaw, the Secretary took 'Lights out'. She looked like a typical Edwardian governess in shirt and blouse, but she had a cheerful voice and I always liked her. A bell got us up in the morning and we went down to Prayers in the gym, followed by breakfast. After about three weeks mother telephoned. An exchange had just been installed in Holt. No private houses were yet connected, but the exchange could be used. Of course, the school had a 'phone as Herts was so much more in the world than Norfolk.

Miss Laura taught me the piano (the advanced instructor was called 'Cat's Meat'). I found the practising periods very handy for indulging in floods of homesick tears. My report at the end of the term was 'Has absolutely no ability for this subject'. I was backward at French and Maths and especially at spelling, which has affected me all my life - now, they call it 'word blindness'. I think that what worried me most was the different dress. I had a blouse and skirt and all the others had smooth cloth tunics and white blouses. The days and weeks passed and the day before we were due to break up, somebody asked me whether I wasn't pleased. I said I was afraid of coming back next term.

We were taken up to London and I was put on the train. I sat at a table and there was an old man sitting opposite me. I ordered tea and ate it all, because we were always hungry at school. The old man smiled at me and said, "Are you satisfied, my dear?"

When I got home, there was hugging all around, and Ponto the Airedale kept jumping up. Even now I was not promoted to going down to dinner but had a tray of food sent to me. I ate the lot and mother exclaimed 'My poor little starveling'. I do not think the Headmistress realised how she was depriving her girls. All the food at school was handed round on dishes for us to help ourselves, but nobody took a big enough helping for fear of being the last to finish and appear greedy. Stupid girls! But silly customs and taboos develop in young communities of one sort or another. My life has been full of surprises.

The long summer holidays passed pleasantly. Tension was somewhat relaxed. Gardeners came back, tennis parties were more frequent and I helped to mow the lawn, by leading the donkey Patrick, who pulled the machine. Khaki disappeared and aspersions were thrown at those who had not worn it. The Germans sank their great fleet to prevent the Allies getting hold of it. The reparations set on that country paved the way to the rise of Hitler. The surprise which struck me most was that as the holidays drew towards an end I did not mind going back to school.

At breakfast the following morning, I was sitting next to a mistress who was pouring out the tea and coffee. I had not seen her before, but I think her name was Keary and she taught English. 'Where do you come from?' she asked. 'Norfolk', I replied. 'Oh, Norfolk! I was there in my teens. My father was agent to Lord Leicester'.

The mind often changes. I was quite glad to go back in the autumn term. There was hockey. It may not have given any satisfaction to anyone else, but it did to me, when I saw my name on the notice board as playing left half for the hockey team the next day. We went to Harrow to play a school there, and lost, but enjoyed it. At this time I was sleeping with another girl called Peggy Graham in a two-room. Some days later I woke up with a stiff neck and could not lift my head, and my companion fetched my breakfast. After a time I felt better and went to see Matron. She was angry with me, but I could not think why. A few days later the headmistress called together the school. The team

41

In the school hockey team.
Jane is third from the right, back row; her future sister-in-law,
Elizabeth Eccles is on the right of the front row.

we had played at Harrow had had cases of diptheria. So that was the reason why the Matron was angry, as she had feared I was getting it.

I was in the Upper study for my last two terms at school, and then my mother offered me the choice of going to Paris to learn French or to a Domestic Science Establishment at Burnham on Sea. I chose the latter, as it was nearer to home. Which was very stupid of me.

After School

On returning home from Burnham there were tennis parties. I was a rabbit at the game. I changed hands, quite the wrong thing to do. This may have been due to my tendency as a young child to have been left-handed. There was a lot of gardening to be done and I worked hard together with the others.

In the early autumn I went with my father and married sister to Jersey. We travelled by night. Next morning we were amongst the islands. Soon, I knew what it was to be seasick and had to go below. Daddy was never seasick at all. We berthed at St Helier, the capital.

Here, the names of the streets are written in French and English. What strikes me most, from distant memory, is the wonderful colour of the rocks and the fury of the incoming tide. Jersey is an attractive island of hill and dale (or was). There are peculiar cabbages with thick stems which grow several feet high and which are made into walking sticks. We bought one and it lasted a year or so. British Income Tax is not paid in Jersey, so at one time many folk flocked there; but now the islanders have got wise to this and only those with substantial incomes are allowed to come.

The Joys of Switzerland

When I was twenty, I went on the Continent with my brother Bobby on a Lee-Francis. We stopped first on a steep hill at Sudbury in Suffolk, and then went on to Canterbury where the streets were decorated, for it was Ascension Day. Over the channel in the steamer to Belgium, and what a contrast! There was a fair going on, and a little stout man holding a clock by the ring at the top was being marched off between two policemen.

We slept the night at Bruges, and the next day went on to Brussels. We lost our way and found we had been round in a circle; when we got the right road it began to rain hard, but we had mackintoshes over us. We spent the night in Alsace; on the way we had several hot drinks of chocolate in pubs.

When we reached the Swiss frontier, we had to show our passports and all our papers. Switzerland was very pretty and hilly. We came to Lucerne and had to go by a steep road by the side of the lake, which was rather dangerous as there were stones rolling down into the lake; however, we got past safely and went on to another lake where we left the motor-bike and walked up to the inn on a mountain called Rigi, by another small lake. At the other side was Mount Pilatus. We had whipped cream and sugar.

The next day we went on southwards and on top of the ridge I saw the most wonderful sight of my life, the main peaks of the Alps stretching away. I determined to go there one day. Eventually we reached the pass, which had a tunnel because it was below the snow line. It took about twenty minutes to get through. We were now in Italy.

The architecture in Switzerland was wooden chalets, but in Italy there were flat-topped houses. We came down to the plain of Lombardy and met up with a procession of mule carts. Some of the drivers were asleep, but they moved to the side to let us pass. Then suddenly the sidecar dropped off the bike with me in it, though I was not hurt. Luckily there was a station nearby and we put the sidecar and bike on to a train and labelled them to be sent home by sea.

We went by train to Venice and stayed at a hotel among the canals and very narrow streets, where we often got lost. I saw squares that were full of pigeons. I heard that a Mr Cator from Norfolk had been so impressed by them that he had sent hampers of them back to Norfolk! We went to an island where they bathed, but I did not fancy a hired bathing dress.

Two days later we decided to stay at a hotel, way up the mountain. It was 5000 feet high and we were the only people there. It was very cold, but luckily there were two beds in my room and I used all the blankets. The next day we proposed to walk across a pass to Austria. When we had got some distance we came to a snow tunnel. While we were waiting, a number of men who had been to a festival at Tionno went into the tunnel and we followed. When we got to the neutral zone between the two countries, we did not have the necessary papers and we had to return by ourselves, only to find that the tunnel had fallen in. We had to walk one at a time between the precipice and the bank of snow. I had only a cotton dress on, and no nailed boots.

We left the hotel the next day, left Austria by train into Germany, and made for the Rhine. We were very hungry as we had not eaten for many hours, so we had a big meal on one of the Rhine steamers. It only cost the equivalent of 2s 9d because of the cruel reparations of the Allies. We reached Cologne in the evening. Bobby found he had forgotten his best suit, which had been left in the hotel in Austria. He was very angry and even blamed me. We spent the night in Cologne and the following day I bought several bottles of Eau-de-Cologne and put them in my overcoat to get through the customs. We left that evening by train for Ostend. I had supper but woke feeling very sick.

There was a rough crossing the next day and I felt quite ill, so I went to a hotel in London to rest.

The following summer I went to Zermatt with mother and Betty Eccles. The latter was an old school friend and destined to become my future sister-in-law. I shared a bedroom with her in the Mount Cervine Annexe and mother slept in the hotel. I woke early the following morning and felt indeed the thrill I had been dreaming about for months, as I watched the sunbeams moving on the chalets outside. Then I fell asleep again and was roused by Betty at a quarter to ten - there was a great rush for breakfast.

We went up to the Riffelalp Hotel, which belonged to the Mount Cervine, mother side-saddle on a hired mule and Betty and I being helped along by holding on to it. It was a misty day and most of the peaks were hidden. On the way back we came to a narrow place and two stout men flattened themselves close to a rock and politely removed their hats. 'That's the King of Holland' said the muleteer. He meant the Prince Regent, for the Queen was staying at Zermatt and came to Dr Fothergill's party's meeting after dinner that night.

Mother and I got out of the train at the last stop before the tunnel through the Alps. A two-wheeled cart was waiting for us in which our luggage was put, and Mother got up by the driver. We had only gone a few yards when one wheel came off. The luggage was put back, but mother preferred to walk with me. We went up a side valley and after a few yards reached the village of Reid. Years ago it had been a popular resort, but now it had faded out of the limelight, except for one hotel, the proprietor of which was a charming man. He arranged for a guide to take me up a mountain the next morning.

It was a lovely day and we walked for some way till we got to the rocks, where the rope was put on. The way was not difficult, and after some time, the guide turned round and held up two fingers, to indicate that we were two minutes from the top. He could only speak German. Suddenly there was an almighty crash. Lightning had hit the summit. The guide turned and rushed down the hill, and I followed as best as I could. At last we got to a large boulder under which we sheltered. The rain fell in torrents and we each muttered in our own language. At last it stopped and we came to pastures, where there were some grasses which the guide picked and indicated that we would make tea. I was worried that mother would be anxious for us, but when we reached Reid there had been no storm there. The next day we went back to the main railway line, and on our way home.

In my early twenties the joys of the beauty of the Alps, and climbing, were never far from my thoughts. For several years I went to Zermatt, once with my elder sister. Bad weather is just as frequent there as in Britain. Then came the first good day for climbing on the Riffelhorn, and a big party set out one fair morning across the snowy glacier. The organiser was Dr Fothergill, who was an expert climber who had a religious bent and was expecting to attend a meeting after dinner that night. The Riffelhorn had many ways up but the easiest was a usual training ground for rock climbing. After about an hour's steady walk on the glacier we let the guide go first. It put me in mind of my childhood, with many branches.

The guide ascends first to a convenient place and belays the spare rope to a rock, and then calls to the next to climb up, and when they are there, then the rest follow. Near the top was a 'chimney', a narrow fissure of steep rock which had to be climbed by wedging yourself up against one side and then climbing with feet and hands on the other The descent was made on the same principle, the guide last.

The winter snow had not all disappeared. I sat with a guide. A paradise of different flowers was on show as I exclaimed in wonder at the surroundings. I had drunk thankfully from the greasy rim of his flask, which had been flattened against a rock to catch the melting snow.

The first fine day at Zermatt I went with several others to climb the Riffelhorn. When we got to the rock, the guide divided us up in fours with a man at the end. Then he climbed up the rock until he came to a safe place and then he called to the next climber on the rope to climb up to him and so on, until we were all together. It was like climbing a big tree. Near the top we came to a chimney, a cleft in the rock. It isascended by pushing one's back to one side of the cleft and clinging to the cleft on the other side with one's hand. On top was a wooden cross which we all reached, cheerful in our accomplishment. When we got to the top we felt very proud of ourselves. We came down in reverse

Cutting steps near the summit of Oberrothom

order with the guide at the back. I was very thirsty when we got down and lay down and drank from a stream, first making sure there were no sheep grazing nearby. The guide and I sat down on a carpet of many coloured flowers. I said to the guide 'How beautiful it is'. He replied, "Ah: but it is because you have been in rock and snow which makes it better still'.

At Zermatt on another occasion, I decided to climb the Riffelhorn by a more difficult route. A young woman of about my own age asked if she could come with me and share the cost of the guide. Of course, I said 'Yes'. Her name was Alice Ward. We set out together and I was just about to put on the rope when I jumped off a rock and the injury to my left knee which I had received at hockey happened again. Of course, I could not go on, but there was no reason why the others should not. When they had gone, I watched the avalanches pour off the summit of Mount Lyscamm, a most dangerous mountain - but I suppose someone has braved it. It was a painful walk back to Zermatt.

We started for Welincooper about 6.30 p.m. to sleep at the Thrift Hut. On the way we had Alexander the guide smiling all over his face, calling out that he had been up the Mettelhorn and was now 'To Let'. It was very chilly at the Thrift Hut. Betty, Joan Cockridge and I shared a room. There were ten of us altogether, including two women who joined us, six guides and a porter. The Hotel had forgotten to send our dinner so we had to buy it, but we were all shivering with cold and as soon as we had finished, we ran about trying to get warm. I had on a vest, a pair of wool combinations, a silk blouse and two sweaters, but it was still cold and I had little sleep. We got up at about 2 a.m. and had some breakfast, which cheered me up considerably. Then Jack Storr arrived. He had walked up from Zermatt to save the expense. He was feeling very mountain sick, but some coffee saved the situation, contrary to Dr Fothergill's gloomy forebodings. He went to the summit and down.

It was a gorgeous moonlit night. The clear cold was exhilarating. The mountains looked fine. The clouds had rolled away except for a few stray slivers of silver. For some time we walked up a fairly good path over moraine. At length we stopped and ate on a rock by a glacier. Dr Fothergill said he could take one more for the Trifthorn and a girl of 17 went.

This is a more difficult climb than the Matterhorn. We roped and started across the glacier. Felix was the guide with Joan, Mr Cockridge and lastly the little porter. A bitter wind from the glacier swept powdered snow in our faces. I had socks on my hands but they soon became so numb that I could hardly feel the rope. Then I collapsed in the snow but the guide pulled me up and gave me some hot coffee and peppermint. He yodelled beautifully and cheered up my spirits. I felt better and we went on again. The glacier became very steep but we went on again, now the last rope. There were good deep footsteps cut. It was the most desolate eternal snow I had ever been on, no glimpses of green valley or vegetation, snow heaped on snow and jagged peaks. Fresh snow on the Matterhorn. In about one and a half hours from the rocks we reached snow again. We were determined to regain our position, instead of resting with the others.

The return journey was without incident. The guide said that I should soon be able to climb the Matterhorn if I had more practice and did not get so tired. We reached Zermatt about 4 pm. I said to myself, 'Blow it! I'm going to have a bath and go into the tea gardens' because there was a long wait till supper.

On returning to England, I went to a specialist who told me that my torn cartilage must come out. I had never had an anaesthetic and was very frightened. I lay in bed shivering. It is said that this is to promote warmth, but I do not know if it is true! However, all went well, though it was painful when I came round. I stayed in the nursing home for about a fortnight in the roar of London. Oh, how I should hate to live in London! Holt is called a town; it is an insult to call it a village, yet it has increased to several thousand since the war; but the houses are largely empty for few can afford to buy.

After leaving London I went to stay with an aunt who lived in Bath for further treatment. I took lessons in diving but made a poor job of it. I bathed in the Roman bath, but this is no longer allowed. When my aunt came down into the town, which is in a hollow, she came in a Bath chair, a curious vehicle which is pulled from the front. I don't know if they persist today or if taxis have taken over. My aunt, who was a sufferer from arthritis, was determined that things should be just so. I hadn't a handbag, only a blue cigarette case, and when escorting her I hung behind, dashed into a shop and bought a blue bag.

My aunt lived in St James Square, near to Regent Square. The former had haunted houses which were unoccupied. Doubtless they have got over the haunting by now. In the Crescent, two sheep fed, and lived out their lives in peace. They know nothing now of a haunted house, I guess.

Joan of Arc

Miss Keary got a commission to write a book on Joan of Arc and she asked Betty Eccles and me to go with her to France. I had not known Betty well at school at Highfield, but what I knew I liked. We met at Victoria Station and as usual I had my bout of sea sickness crossing the

49

channel. Most of our travelling was done by train, we had to hire a taxi now and again. Betty and I shared a bedroom. We went to Domrémy where Joan was born and spent her childhood. Her people were peasant farmers, and it was here that she first heard her voices. France was being continually harassed by the English, who said they had lands and privileges there. The French Dauphin was peace-loving and disinclined to oppose aggression, it must be said. Joan left Domrémy never to return again to her home. At the time I went to France, she was in the limelight again as she had just been canonised by the Catholic Church of Rome. A little nun at Domrémy asked Miss Keary whether it was true that protestants worshipped the good God!

For some strange reason my interest in Joan was not much stirred. I ate buns soaked in rum till I sickened myself of them! There was much to talk about between the three of us, which was interesting and soothing and had a salutory effect on my personality. It was a calm crossing on the return journey and I was not sick for the first time. Later in the year I went to stay with Miss Keary in her north London flat, which she kept for her niece Ruth, who had a job. Miss Keary let me go about London alone and I happened on the Lord Mayor's Show. A resplendent individual who looked as though he ought to be sitting upright at the back of the coach was leaning half out of the window and doffing his hat to the cheering crowds.

I don't know how the subject came up, and I'm going back to our travels in France, Miss Keary said to us, 'I shall die in 1939'. She did! In the south of France where somebody had sent her for a change.

In the late 1930's, Miss Keary, now retired, came round to stay. We took her in the car to Walsingham Church. Afterwards, she said 'May I see the Church of England now?' 'That was it' we replied. She shook her head. 'I thought it was Roman Catholic!'

A few days after Miss Keary left to stay with relatives at Rudham, I went on a visit to Dorothy Baxter at Grimsby. Travelling by the old Midland and Great Northern Railway I passed through Rudham and Miss Keary got in my carriage. When I told her I was going to stay with Dorothy she mumbled 'rather dull'. However I quite enjoyed myself going inland through the rolling green wolds, and the Fish Market where there were curious specimens including cat fish which had whiskers like four legs.

50

I was busy enough at home, gardening, taking Mother shopping and occasionally playing golf at Sheringham or Blakeney. I had bought an open Austin car second-hand and learned to drive it. No driving test then. It answered me for a short time but Mother insisted on my buying a better car, and I got a new Austin 7 for £120. Even then, it was not the cheapest. As to the old car, it was used in a scene of a Red Cross War Office Inspection, turned over on its side as if there had been an accident, and a Boy Scout lay underneath. Oil dripped on his face and on an old mac he wore.

The General Strike

The basic cause of the General Strike of 1926 was that Britain's economy was in a mess because she had relied on pre-war markets which were now lost. Wages were low, and unemployment high. In assessing its more immediate cause it is advisable to glance at the politics of the time.

At the General Election of 1923 the Tories had such a small majority over other parties that the King, George V, without more to-do called on Ramsey Macdonald to form the first Labour Government. He only held office for one year, one reason being the Prime Minister's intervening in trying to stop the prosecution of the editor of the *Daily Worker*. For this editor had allowed the publication of an article inciting the army not to obey orders against strikers.

Four days before the election the *Daily Mail* published the famous Zinoviev Letter which was supposed to come from the Communist International urging the unemployed to form themselves into Communist cells. Even the Government seemed to have been taken in at first by this letter which was indeed a hoax. But it had an influence on the General Election when the Tories had a majority and Stanley Baldwin became Prime Minister.

It was miners who had the greatest grievances, and this industry badly needed better terms. There had been hunger marches from Glasgow and Paisley to London. It was part of the Trades Union Conference, but behaved in rather a provocative manner during the prolonged negotiations between the TUC and the Government. No agreement was reached and on May 3rd 1926 the General Strike began.

Now let us glance at Norwich. The population was then 126,000. At the last census of 1988 it was 171,300. At the time of the earlier one it had the second highest rates in the country owing to the poor relief. The boot and shoe industry did not strike, neither did the Post office.

To digress, the newspapers of that date had much smaller print than today and good eyes were needed to read it. The weekly papers, such as the Holt Post, which served the neighbourhood, had much more national news in it than the equivalent today, for many could not afford a daily paper. Friday, the day of its publication, was known as 'paper reading night'. The following appeared in it on May 11th. The Lord Mayor of Norwich during the first day's stoppage, walked through the streets talking frankly and sincerely man to man: 'We have survived worse things than this and we shall win through. But we must all keep steady and see the other fellow's point of view.'

Thorpe station next morning was a home of ineffable peace. Lines of carriages stood at the platforms. Mr Wilson, the Station Master, was at his post. Other officials chatted affably with would-be passengers and men who appeared to be strikers. No trains were running. The bookstall man and the cigar kiosk girl were monarchs of the scene. One munched a sandwich in the almost deserted refreshment room and reflected on the inscrutable way of us who wage a fight which the whole world is watching with as much unconcern as men of other nations would light a cigarette. A man in uniform was standing in the station hall speaking with rather a fervid man who may have been a striker. The station cat, wondering whence the unwonted peace, rubbed its head against their legs. Uniform picked him up, stroked his head. We are wonderful people!

Nationally, the TUC had agreed not to use violence in the conduct of the strike but it had a militant minority to contend with. In London, bus windows were protected with wire netting against stone throwing. But in Norwich there were good relations between the strikers and the police. The 200 special constables who had been alerted were not called upon; football matches between police and strikers took place on Mousehold Heath and on the old ground at the Nest. On the first day of the strike, 100 volunteers were ready to do tasks usually performed by those on strike, but no trams were running. Boys played football in the streets, but that was nothing unusual in those days of comparatively small traffic.

Let us look at the country districts of Norfolk through the lines of a local weekly newspaper. In the country districts work went on as usual, and little, or no interest was manifested by rural workers in the strike about them and they did their jobs in the usual way. (The farm workers had their strike two years previously.) The absence of newspapers appeared to be the most regretted feature and the BBC bulletins morning, afternoon and evening were eagerly awaited and listened to. The problem of getting fish supplies to market from the east coast towns presented some difficulty, but a certain number of fish, crabs and lobsters were dispatched by road to Norwich.

I kept a diary at the time of the General Strike. On May 2nd my mother received instructions as to what to do in case of future contingencies. When the strike began at midnight on the 3rd May the BBC gave out five bulletins daily. I listened avidly, but all I had was a crystal set and ear-phones. I had to scratch about with the needle in order to hear. It was reassuring when I heard in a strong cheerful voice the familiar 'This is London calling'. During the strike the BBC was less biased than the few newspapers which appeared. The Government published a couple of sheets called the *British Gazette.* One morning I drove the mail bag from Holt to Norwich in the family car with my mother. I covered it up with rugs in case we were stopped by strikers, but nothing happened, and we returned via Melton Constable with the mail for that railway village, and another for Holt. Though the Post office was not on strike the mail vans were not running, and the delivery of letters was dependant on private cars.

On Thursday May 29th, the General Strike was called off by all except the miners, who continued for some months. Stanley Baldwin appeared in the doorway of Number Ten, and took off his bowler to the crowds. I was secretly and selfishly rather sorry. It had been an excitement in rather a dull life.

Red Cross

In the 1930's there was a great deal of herring fishing by Scottish trawlers from Great Yarmouth. Girls came from Scotland to do the gutting and salting of the fish for export. So doing, they got sores on their hands. The Red Cross bought an old dressing station to treat the girls in, each day as they finished their work, and they had changed and were clean. Three members of the Red Cross came weekly during the first year, staying at the YWCA. There was a trained nurse in charge as well as a Commandant to help keep the books. The first year we agreed to have our own celebration at the end of the week, we brought coffee and food etc. for a party after the fishing girls had gone home to their lodgings. We did not foresee the consequences; the manager of the YWCA was furious at our not being home before midnight, and she said she would report us to headquarters, which she did, but all that happened was that we each received a polite letter saying it was rather late for us to be out at night when working so hard.

The next year the Red Cross took over an empty hotel and staffed it with volunteers and a full time cook, the members got the chance to go to the dressing station once or twice. The busiest time was always November when I asked to go. In the daylight hours we attended the fishermen who were not able to go out in the trawlers because of boils, due to an unbalanced diet. I remember one who had a bad boil and had been in hospital saying 'I would rather be in among the whales and the fishes than in one of them places.'

On the first floor of the dressing station there was a rest room for the Scottish visitors where they did some fine singing. The girls would not have got sore fingers if they had worn gloves when working, but they refrained because it slowed them up. The Red Cross went for weekly sessions during the period when the North Sea was being over-fished. Herring was so cheap they were used to manure the fields.

James Pointer

Some years before, a neighbour had pinched our gardener and a message was brought in that another man was waiting for interview. Mother said to go and see him. This was James Pointer. 'How old are you?' I asked. 'Forty' he replied with a wink. 'I was here with your grandfather'.

Pointer became one of the most important people. He came from his cottage by bicycle and worked until he had finished a job, no matter how late it was. He came in one day, leaned his bike against the stables and said 'My wife died in the night'. I said, 'I'm so sorry, Pointer'. 'What will be will be' he murmured, and went about his jobs. He kept the garden in good order. When I wanted wreaths made, he would make them. I never told him what to do, but I was alarmed when he put a ladder up against the high stable door and began to paint it, in spite of our efforts to stop him. At length he got down for something. Mrs Girdwood who was watching rushed out and got the ladder and put it in the drawing room. Pointer was very angry and told her to bring it back. Mrs Girdwood brought him a new pair of long-handled clippers. Pointer was angry even though he did not show it.

I used to fetch and take him back in the car, sometimes round to do other errands. When I took him to Sheringham he went and took some cuttings from the churchyard while I was in the dentist. Having no wife he had to have a housekeeper; she had some funny turns so was brought with him to the garden. One morning I had a message to say Pointer was not well. I went down there immediately and found him in bed. 'I'm not going to stay here very long' he said. 'I'm going to fly out of that window'. He died the next day. He was 92 years old. I was very moved at his funeral in Glandford Church and could not attend a service there for months afterwards. I remember him saying once when he called 'I'm working now on a garden which ain't big enough for two pigeons to play in!' He was devoted to dogs and said nothing when it was pointed out that one was lying on a seed bed.

Boy Scouts and Wolf Cubs

I well remember how it started. My father had been having a game of bowls and all the other players had had tea and gone, except the Rector, the Revd A. J. King. He said to me, 'Would you consider starting a pack of Wolf Cubs?' I said 'Yes' immediately. About ten boys volunteered, mostly from Church Street.

I went over to see Avis Marsh who had the Scouts and Cubs. She showed me how to do the Grand Owl. After a meeting or two I said we would have a great hunting day. Unfortunately it clashed with a school outing to the seaside and the boys also wanted to go to that. I was very angry and said they could all leave. A few days later the organiser of the Wolf Cubs for the County came over. When I told her what I had done, she was aghast and said she would try and get them back. They learned to tie knots and skip, and I had them by turn in the kitchen at my home. The Cook said, 'Oh, I do like knot-tying'. I said 'Why?' and she replied 'It is better than sitting in the kitchen'. The Cook went on to say that she dare not leave them alone, they might do any sort of mischief; they might open the face of the clock.

Cawston and Holt Scouts in the garden at Holt, about 1935

The following year I took them to an old School House to camp for four days. I slept in a tent outside. The boys could not go to sleep, and when I dropped off I was awakened by them, and felt so very tired the following day. We cooked over a trench fire. The next night they all slept soundly. When it came to going home, they all felt proud of themselves.

In April the green of Sandringham Park is decked with groups of daffodils, and here is the neat bungalow of Mrs Ambrose. She wears a collar around her neck for she suffers from arthritis. Her father was a loader for King Edward VII.

Sandringham House has a flower show on the last Wednesday in July, but there was not a show when I took the mother of one of my scouts to see Mrs Ambrose, who told us that Prince John used to come and see her, with his governess. He was a nice boy, but delicate, and died when he was fifteen. When the scout's mother saw Prince John's stone in the churchyard she said 'That there stun put me in mind of a piece of pork cheese. I like a piece of pork cheese, if I know where it has come from'.

In the following summer the Colonel of a Territorial Battalion asked the Holt Detachment to send members to the Weybourne Camp in case there were accidents with the guns. The Commandant, Q, Cook, myself and about four members went. We had a spot by ourselves, a large mess tent. Every month a civilian aeroplane was flown from the Mousehold Airfield in Norwich by a young man from Weybourne to use as a mock target and for sound detection. The pilot said he would like to take up two VAD's, and I was one who went. We were just aloft when he offered us a packet of 'Players' - there was a notice in the plane saying 'No Smoking'.

We flew back to Norwich and then returned to Weybourne; then we went from Aylsham to Weybourne about five times before returning to Mousehold. After that flying, the sister of my companion was sitting in her garden at St Faiths, just outside Norwich. She said an aeroplane had gone over dangerously low.

The following summer we went to a camp at Cleever in Cornwall, nearly a 300-mile drive in my car. Marjorie Pearson went with me as

Cook, but had migraine for two days after, probably brought on by the journey. There were large cliffs here, and the bathing was dangerous. The soldiers were very friendly, bathing, but lads are too foolhardy and could not be relied on to keep to the foam of the waves in the small bay. I left my camp equipment for the next Commandant except for my tent - but the next fortnight war broke out and I lost it all.

Hitler's War

On the outbreak of Hitler's war, September 3rd, 1939, children from London were sent by sea to Yarmouth. On landing there was an air raid alarm and they were crowded together in a churchyard. Some had head lice or nits, and they spread them amongst most of the others. The alarm proved to be a false one. When the children were distributed about the county, the infection could not be left entirely to the foster parents to treat, so volunteers collected them at centres and cleaned their heads. My first job was doing this with a wire comb and disinfectant.

The phoney war continued through the Autumn with a battalion of troops being billeted in Holt. Just after the new Year of 1940 I had a message from the Colonel saying there was a 'flu epidemic amongst his men, and would like us (the Red Cross Detachment) to nurse some of the cases in the local Church Hall. Soldiers scrubbed the Hall and before they had finished the first cases were brought in. Beds had been borrowed, and the patients brought with them their Army blankets. Cooking was done for them on a gas stove and I was surprised that even men with high temperatures relished their food. The patients had only their ordinary shirts and wool 'Long Johns' to sleep in, and when they got up their figures resembled ballet dancers. After dark it was very stuffy in the hall as owing to the blackout, windows and shutters had to be kept closed. Ventilation was bad for about 25 men.

After some days a 'Brass hat' arrived and ordered our patients to better accommodation at Norwich and Stiffkey. However, this was easier said than done, as deep snow and hard frost had set in. Two ambulances with patients and VAD's in attendance set off and got to their destination but owing to drifts could not return. So we kept the hall open and also a room at the Feathers Hotel for 17 days.

Soon after this, help was needed in the Weybourne Camp Hospital. The camp was then occupied by the ill-fated 5th Battalion, Royal Norfolk Regiment which was later sent to Singapore, where the men were taken prisoners by the Japanese. There was still deep snow. The war winters of 1939-40, 1940-41,1941-42 were all very cold in Norfolk. I had to get to Weybourne through the deep snow in an old Austin 7. There was German measles at Weybourne as well as 'flu. After a time, things improved and my help was no longer needed, and I got German measles.

After Weybourne, I nursed for a time at Kelling Sanatorium which was then for TB cases only. One of the patients was a young RAF officer with a tendency to the complaint. I met him on June 17th, when the collapse of France was imminent. He greeted me with 'Good, now they will take me back into the RAF'.

My mother had gone to stay with her sister in Staffordshire owing to the invasion threat. The boys of Gresham's School were moved to Newquay, and troops occupied the building. The coastal Rural Districts of Norfolk were banned except for those living there and their relations, and persons on urgent business.

I went to work at the Red Cross Hospital in the old Hall in the park at Woodbastwick. Sometimes, when I was off duty in the morning, I went across Horning Ferry to have coffee at the Hotel. Broadland seemed deserted by visitors and boats. It was silent except for the sound of bursting bombs in the distance, for German aeroplanes came in from the sea and dropped their loads. One night afterwards the Ferry Inn got a direct hit from a bomb. It was crowded with servicemen and others, and many were killed and injured.

Whilst I was at Woodbastwick a German aeroplane came along and hit the laundry near the hospital with shrapnel. Patients were carried into outside trenches, one on a special bed. (He was said to be the first casualty in Norfolk, and had been at a searchlight base). Though he could not move, when a stretcher was placed by his bed he got out with ease. Soon the aeroplane flew away.

I went back to Holt earlier than I expected owing to the invasion scare, but after the success of the Battle of Britain this receded. Hitler had made one of his mistakes aiming his bombs on London - brave but poor metropolis!

One June night I was awakened by the loudest noise I had ever heard about 1.15 am. I put on my siren suit and went up to an attic facing south. In the distance I saw smoke rising. I went outside and met some Wardens. They were looking where the 'bomb' had fallen and I told them where I thought it was, about half a mile to the south of Holt in a field near the Norwich road. It proved to be a land mine. These were always dropped in pairs, and the other one fell on an empty house. Glass blew out of the windows in Holt and splinters fell on people sleeping in bed, but no one was hurt, in spite of the shock waves. The crater which I saw was about 15 ft deep and 15 - 20 ft wide.

At the beginning of the war when it was comparatively peaceful in Norfolk, somebody remarked, 'Hitler has a rod in pickle for Norwich.' He was right. In the so-called 'Baedeker' raids (the name was taken from a well-known guidebook), the Germans turned their attention on historic cities. Norwich was attacked on April 27th and 28th, 1943. The first raid began with the dropping of parachute flares. The city had not been so illuminated since the Diamond Jubilee. Then followed a silver rain of incendiary bombs, some of which fell on the Cathedral, but the Grammar School boys climbed up and threw them off before they exploded. A Mobile Unit of volunteers was stationed at Colman Road. It consisted of a Doctor, trained Nurse, and four male and female others. One of them told me the whole city seemed to be burning, and smelt of smoke, soot, and explosive. An old man in a lighted doorway called out to them 'Help my wife' as they drove past, but they could not stop, as they had been ordered to the Heigham Road district. Near the Dolphin Inn a shelter had been hit and most of the occupants were killed or severely hurt. The noise was terrific. Heard from 20 miles away, it seemed as though nothing could survive in Norwich.

The bombardment went on for one and a half hours. Bowthorpe Hospital for old people was hit, and part of the Norfolk and Norwich Hospital was put out of action. One of the patients had left his false teeth in a ward, and a nurse went back to retrieve them. Houses, churches, and ancient buildings crumbled, 162 people were killed and 600 injured. The following night Norwich was attacked again, mostly with incendiary bombs, and 69 were killed and 89 seriously wounded.

At this time there was a First Aid Point in every village in the Erpingham District Council area, and I was an instructor in Air Raid Precautions, and used to give talks. On dark nights it was difficult to find the way to some First Aid Points. All finger-post signs had been removed on the outbreak of war, and lights on cars had to be dim. If a car was left standing without the driver, the distributor head had to be taken away by the driver. One night at Gresham I released some tear gas for practice with respirators at the end of a session. After a few minutes I opened the door for the gas to clear, but the wind was blowing in and it would not disperse. Adjoining was a room where the Home Guard slept, and I had an anxious time waiting for the gas to go.

A battalion of soldiers occupied the Gresham's School houses at Holt whilst two other battalions were on coastal defence. They changed over monthly. In the old School House there were rest quarters for men who were unwell and they were looked after by Red Cross members and orderlies. This continued till July 1944 when the last soldiers left Holt and the Gresham's boys came back to their School houses. Holt was its old self again.

In June 1944 the 'buzz bombs' started dropping on London. These were powered by engines which stopped, allowing the bomb to fall and explode. I was asked by the Red Cross if I could find a house suitable for a hostel for asthmatic children from London. I heard of a fine Georgian House at Letheringsett belonging to the Cozens-Hardy family, who agreed to lend it. On August Bank Holiday my old gardener and myself began cleaning the house, which had been occupied by solders. Within a week the asthmatic children and the beds arrived, all within seven hours. In all we had 21 children, mostly boys, between the ages of 6 and 13. We were lucky in finding a young and pretty assistant nurse from Beckham Infirmary, and the children loved her, and were not at all homesick. Older children walked up the hill to Holt school daily. In the yard behind the house was a picturesque long-fronted shed. In this we put four 'Elsans'. One day I noticed the pipes were missing. The boys had taken them to make tunnels in the wild garden, but generally they were very well-behaved. The Hostel was open for a year and a month, when the children went back to London, sorry to leave.

Red Cross Detachment at Children's Hostel, Letheringsett, 1944-5

I was driving along the road between Swaffham and Brandon when I passed a garden full of pheasant eye narcissus which I stopped to admire, upon which the man standing in the garden gave me a bag of bulbs.

The village of Mundford is off the main road. I found a small house darkened by shrubs. A woman was lying stretched out on a bed by the window. I tapped on the door and went in. She had been notified to us by a very important person outside the county as being able to repair old lace. Her father had had a post in the Tower of London. Now she was alone in the world, suffering from some rare disease. An apparatus with a lead going down her back was fixed to the wall, and she was taken up to a London hospital at times for treatment. Mrs Morris from the next county had said she would look after the case. All sorts of rumours were about. People said she went out early in the morning to pinch potatoes, and had been had up before the 'beak'; then something happened and she broke her thigh, and was moved to a nursing home in Norwich and was found to be well off. Mr and Mrs Morris went to clean up the house. They found in one room stocks of raisins, butter and stale food. She was a hoarder. In the nursing home she had her little pile of oddments. Mrs Morris went to visit her until she died.

Mrs Girdwood

I have not yet spoken of Mrs Girdwood, who befriended me at the time of the Second World War. She was almost continually my helper and companion. She was born on Vancouver Island, but was brought to this country by her family to be educated. When the war broke out she joined the WVS. Hers was a familiar figure in Holt, wearing a green Burberry and a green WVS hat. She had a room in Harworth House owned by the Misses West, Daisy and Kitty.

Her great task and contribution to the war effort was her service to the volunteers from Newfoundland. She ended her day by walking 2 1/2 miles to Hunworth Rectory where there was a big Naval gun with Newfoundland volunteers. These men were volunteers, not conscripts, and their officers, who were strangers to the men, made no effort to keep their own officers, and were very dull. It was to Mrs Girdwood they brought all their troubles. Indeed there might have been a mutiny had she not talked to them and sold them sweets, cigarettes and coffee.

At about this time a bull got away from a local farm and roamed the countryside for several weeks. It caused Mrs Girdwood some problems as it was loose in the area that she had to walk through on her daily rounds. No-one could catch it, so it had to be shot. It was not always the right people who got the recognition for what they did in the war. Mrs Girdwood did not. Only once was their big Naval gun fired. The shell landed a few miles from Wells. Nearly all the windows in nearby Hunworth were broken. The residents all crowded into the Commanding Officer's quarters demanding compensation. She had a son who was reported missing, but eventually it was found that he was a prisoner of war in North Africa.

The Misses West were ageing, so they moved into a smaller house in Holt, but Mrs Girdwood moved with them and looked after them. One day she went with me in my car to the opening of the Red Cross Club in Dereham. When we were quite near, we saw a man's legs sticking out from under a hedge, so we stopped to see what had happened. We went through the field gate and there was a man apparently unconscious. I spoke to him and he mumbled something - he lived in a village nearby - so we both dragged him to his feet and took him to the village he mentioned. When we stopped at his home, I got out and knocked at the door. A woman opened it. 'Your husband has had an accident', I said. She looked at him and said quite angrily, 'That he hasn't, he's dead drunk. You should have left him where he was'. We were late for the opening of the Club.

One day in Holt I saw her outside a Wine Merchant's talking to a ragged-looking woman. After a few minutes she went inside the shop, and came out with a bottle of brandy, which she gave to the woman, who was profuse in her thanks.

Mrs Girdwood died in 1968 and was much mourned. Her milestone-like memorial is within the coping of the Hales grave in the churchyard.

After two years Daphne got a Council flat in what had been the station at the end of our old seven acre field and I needed a housekeeper. I let this be known and a couple with a young girl came to the door, they did not appeal to me and I said no. However I heard that they had a job at Letheringsett Hall old people's home so I went to see them there. They were living in a caravan leaking with icicles hanging down inside so I took pity on them and told them to come. They stayed several years and were not satisfactory - Mrs Morson was no worker - in hot weather she would sit in a shady place in the garden doing nothing or indoors where she would sit gossiping to a friend and eating cream cakes. Her husband was alcoholic and went to Kelling Hospital to be dried out. The girl grew into a most unpleasant teenager who would not speak to me.

I had always been attracted by peacocks since the old Rodbaston days and I bought a pair of peacocks and peahens. Their hut was in two sections so that when the grass got too short they could be transferred to the other side, which had been reseeded. Their wild call was the first to be heard in the morning but there were never any complaints. I got rid of them after a few years because of the difficulty of feeding them in the winter. I shed a few tears though I knew they were going to a big open place where they would be happier.

At last I could put up with the Morsons no longer. Next year I had a family called Traggett. Mrs Traggett, a handsome woman, had multiple sclerosis and soon had to take to her bed, her mother, 'Granny', had to come and look after her and the young children, a boy called Tommy who was just beginning to talk and a girl about five. Mr Traggett had a small farm and a partner. He worked hard for a time then damped off and did nothing. He was no help or comfort to his wife. I liked and was sorry for Granny - she was having to sleep in an attic, but I lent her one of my spare rooms. Later Traggett had to sell up his farm, he married a woman he had been courting and brought her home. After her daughter's funeral, Granny came to me, and later, Tommy, who was neglected and was having bouts of sickness. Every weekend he came here and Granny spoilt him, but that was not to be wondered at. Looking after her daughter had tired her head. We were happy together for several years.

One summer day Granny had made a lovely bowl of flowers for the dining room grate. After a good supper I went to bed. I was just going to sleep when Granny came into my room saying she felt awful, and collapsed by my bed - I rang the doctor but by the time he had come, she had died. With my dog I went to sit in the dining room. The flowers she had done were radiant, and she was no more.

A couple came very shortly in their sixties. They were from a very lonely place - 2 1/2 miles to the shop. I took to them immediately. The wife had worked for one of the Ministers in Norwich for seventeen years and her husband had been a shepherd and on the land.

The next few years were happy ones for me - Mrs Girdwood was my mainstay and my clerical work kept me busy. The need for occupation for the disabled in the County kept me out and about. Mrs Arnott and Mrs Ringer both taught home cases and I attended to their other various needs. Mrs Girdwood and her landladies moved from their big old house to a much smaller modern one near a garage. It was more a case of Mrs G looking after them, but she was mostly with me. She was noticeably ageing, with loss of memory, and was a bit fractious. James her son often came and was aware of her decline. Then her leg swelled. She didn't remember anything I said, after five minutes. Eventually she went to Cromer Hospital where they operated on her and found a cancer, but they had to leave the tumour in. I went to see her every day. After a few days I was telephoned just after I had had lunch to say that she was gone.

A Letter Surprise

First the New Year Honours in the Press and readers scanning them to see if they know any of the recipients. Then the investitures in February of which little is heard.

On a November morning Alice had a letter marked 'On Her Majesty's Service'. Alice sighed; no doubt it was from the Tax people or of that ilk. Then she got the surprise of her life; it was from the Prime Minister asking if she would accept an MBE. It put Alice's mind in a whirl so she went upstairs and had a bath.

When February came, Alice, with a friend caught the train from Norwich to Liverpool Street Station, where they met another friend for two passes had been issued for the investiture on the morrow. They went to a hotel overlooking a park for the night.

Alice woke early before dawn. Through the window she saw lights spread far away, a single bright star above and in the park the dark silhouettes of bare trees. Alice had her breakfast in bed and went downstairs. It was almost time to be off so she asked the hall porter to get a taxi. The first driver said 'I'm not going there, there's an investiture on - too much traffic'. Alice waited impatiently. At last a taxi stopped at the door and Alice and her friends got in. It was sunny but very cold; they went through Trafalgar Square and into the inner quadrangle of Buckingham Palace. Alice, in her agitation, gave the taxi driver a tip out of all proportion.

Having shown their passes to an official, they went to the entrance of the Palace where it was very warm. They were greeted by a slim young man in tails with a single medal on a white ribbon on his coat. He directed Alice's friends in one direction and Alice in another. Alice with her guide walked along a red carpeted corridor with sofas on one side below the windows. The young man attached something that looked like a curtain hook to her jacket, and she sat down by an old man who looked as though he had been poured into his morning suit. He said he was 87 and had to be in Manchester that evening, but Alice did not recognise him as Albert Tatlock of 'Coronation Street' fame.

A band rang out with the National Anthem, the Prince of Wales had arrived. A line of men in morning dress or service uniform began to pass with here and there a woman. 'It's a man's world' said one of Alice's companions on the sofa. Meanwhile, the band played with some songs from Gilbert and Sullivan, but Alice could not see into the vast ballroom.

After about an hour, the slim young man beckoned to Alice to join the file, and as she moved round the corner of the corridor she could see the ballroom where the Prince stood in naval uniform. Alice curtseyed, and the Prince, seeing that she was lame and had a stick, gave her his hand. 'Where do you come from?' he asked. Alice told him. 'You must have done a lot for the Red Cross', he said. Alice in her embarrassment made a gaff. She just said 'Yes Sir' when she ought to have replied, 'Many have done more'.

It was all over in a minute. Alice passed to a small room where a man was sitting at a table. He took off her medal and curtain hook, and gave Alice back the former in a case. She was led into the ballroom and sat down on a gilt chair. Now she could see the whole scene. Behind her were the tiers of spectators, in front a great space up to the dais. Some motionless figures were dotted about. Alice marvelled that they could stand so long like statues, and thought one or other would fall down flat in a faint but nothing happened. Behind the Prince on the dais was a semi-circle of Beefeaters in scarlet Tudor dress with coloured rosettes on the shoes, and flowers wreathing their hats. Beefeaters prefer to be called Yeomen of the Guard and date from Henry VII's reign. Now they are recruited from sergeants of the regular army with good reputation and physique.

The National Anthem again, and the show was over. Alice found her friends and they walked past a file of dismounted Household Cavalry with drawn swords; they were so rigid Alice thought for a second they were dummies! At the entrance, the slim young man handed them to a Scotsman in a kilt. It was bitterly cold outside. Everyone was seeking taxis. Alice stood by a policeman at the gates of the quadrangle, who wanted to shut them. In the nick of time a taxi drew up, and Alice and her friends got into its comparitive warmth.

Back at the hotel, Alice sank into a chair. The pomp and the pageantry of the Palace was still on her mind but it had been an ordeal. 'Here's a sherry for you', said someone.

Once in a lifetime

I was brought up on the tale of the 1897 flood at Salthouse. 'Once in a lifetime, that come.' I heard many details about it from old Salthouse people later. How Ruth and her family were having breakfast that November morning and looked out over the marsh, '. . . when all on a sudden, that come slopping over.' Ruth laughed, but her husband said, 'You may well laugh.' Before long the water was in the house, carrying away the cinders hissing from the fire. Ruth and her children went out at the back to higher land and stayed with her relations 'come Valentine'. They called it 'The Rage' in those days.

It was a very windy day on January 31st 1953 when a Holt shopkeeper remarked, 'The sea will be through tonight.' Sure enough, I was sitting by the fire about 6 o'clock when the telephone rang. It was Nurse Docking from Cley and she said, 'There is some flooding in the village; can you get a canteen?' Immediately, I rang Miss Griffith, then the Red Cross Director, who lived at Morston. She was upstairs, for her ground floor was flooded. She rang the Watton mobile canteen; after that the lines went dead.

Mrs Girdwood and I went down to Cley. The Street was flooded and we had to approach by a higher road above the viallage. There are alleyways leading down to The Street. I only had a small torch, which was nearly exhausted, but I soon smelled petrol and realised I was in the wrong alley. The one I wanted led to the Post Office where there were a number of people trapped upstairs. I tried to reach the correct alleyway but soon got into deep water and had to turn back. There were US airmen in the district and many of their families lodged in Cley. The narrow road was choc-a-bloc with cars, airmen looking for or having found their families. 'Where shall I take my children?' asked one in desperation. Mrs Girdwood suggested Nurse Dockings's house above the village, so off they went and stayed there for six weeks.

Meanwhile the Watton canteen had arrived and a man carried a VAD through the water to the Post Office. There was no light, and the pipes had burst, letting out the sewage. The houses in Cley Street are fitted with tide boards, but the water still overflowed into the houses, and the occupants had to take refuge upstairs, fearful that the whole house might collapse about them. Thinking we had done all we could for the moment, Mrs Girdwood and I went home, telling the canteen staff to follow and we would have a good fire ready for them It was bitterly cold, with a north-west wind. I awoke early, but the staff had still not arrived. Then there was a knock on the door and a friend of mine, Margaret Spurrell, arrived with two dogs. Her house was on the side of the Glaven Valley, backing on to higher land. When the Cley bank broke, the sea rushed up the valley. Margaret retreated upstairs, but, fearing the house was going to collapse, threw the dogs out of the window on the high side, tied sheets together and let herself down to join them. She was lucky, after walking some distance, to get a lift into Holt. I suggested she should go to bed, but she refused, so we shut the dogs into a bedroom; when we returned later to see them, both were asleep with their heads on a pillow!

Mrs Girdwood and I went down to Cley with several helpers. The canteen had been there all night. The Glaven Valley was flooded to the outskirts of Bayfield, and the high arched bridge called 'Nowhere' had disappeared under the flood. Helen Barclay had rescued an old couple living near it. The Valley looked as it must have done in mediaeval times when ships came up to Wiveton. Looking into houses in Cley made one think a giant had been in, with furniture overturned. A woman who did a lot of washing for people from London had placed it in a basket and gone upstairs. All night she feared for the washing; when she came down in the morning, both table and washing had risen up to the ceiling, and the washing was safe!

Salthouse had been even worse hit. Houses collapsed and a woman was drowned. And where had the flock of geese vanished to, at Cley? Suddenly they appeared, buoyant and trim, and gave people quite a boost. Clothes were wanted for victims of the flood, for they had lost almost everything. The Red Cross set about collecting them and there was a depot at Salthouse church, clothes being hung on the screen. Some were so poor and dirty, they had to be burned, which gave rise to a story that the Red Cross were burning the clothes that had been given to them for the flood victims!

A few days later someone told me at Cley of a man who was very ill and had lost his pills in the flood, and urgently required some more from the doctor at Blakeney. Would I go and fetch them? Owing to the flooding of the Valley, I had to go nearly back to Holt in order to get to Blakeney. The doctor was out, but an assistant gave me the pills and I returned to Cley. To get to the man's house, I had to scramble over rubble, as the road was still flooded. When I eventually reached the house, a woman greeted me. 'What did you want to bother with them for? They're only his 'perients, and there be some more on the mantelpiece. I fetched them out of the flood!'

A man at Salthouse told me that on returning home about 5.30, the marshes were clear, but at 6 o'clock, the door was pushed open and in swam the dog!

There has been only one very minor flood since then. I went to Cley to inspect and there was only shallow water in The Street, though the coast road was flooded. I went on to Salthouse, where the policeman on duty advised me to return to Holt and find somewhere to house the inhabitants of cottages which were threatened with flood water. This I did, and fixed up for the Church Hall to be used. But in that short time the tide had started to recede, and the inhabitants did not have to leave their homes after all.

Branch Welfare Officer

After Hitler's War Mrs Girdwood and I went to sort out the equipment in a big Hall off the Aylsham Road in Norwich for Mrs Browne the Red Cross County Secretary. One cold day I asked her, jokingly, if we could use some splints to make a fire. She said 'Yes, certainly' so I did. About this time, Mr Sargeant the County Director asked me whether I would start and run a Welfare Department. I agreed, but heard no more about it, so after a while I rang up. Mr Sargeant hesitated and said 'We did not know if you were qualified enough.' I was very disappointed but the next day received a letter from National Headquarters to the effect that I had been appointed Welfare Officer for the County, so in effect I had been approved.

In the earlier days of my term as Branch Welfare Officer we arranged social clubs for the disabled at which an instructor, Mrs Ringer, taught handwork. Once a year in the summer we had a rally at a different place and the club with the best exhibits won a cup for a year. There was a small club at Hunstanton and a big one at Aylsham, and others. Now, I fear, they have all disappeared. One thing that is the same, and just as good now is the Medical Loan of which Elizabeth is in charge, and supplies all the county through the depots and centres. The handwork is sold at the Sandringham Flower Show. If the makers have paid for the material they get the profit; if not it goes to the Red Cross Branch. Each year the takings go up, but this may be due to inflation, for I don't think there is such a varied display as there used to be. One year a man from South Lynn made little coloured windmills on stakes for frightening birds off seed beds. They were so pretty.

Sandringham

There seems a gap between the end of the last war and the present, but a thread which binds them together is Sandringham. In April, Sandringham Park is very green with splashes of daffodils, but by the time of the Flower Show on the last Wednesday in July, the turf is worn down by the putting up of the tents. I used to go there with the Handcrafts teachers to see if we could sell anything of their work. On

71

one occasion, fortunately I went early and found our marquee had neither tables nor chairs! I had to work long to borrow some. It was not until 11 o'clock that the Royal Standard went up and we knew the Queen Mother was on the Ground. We put on our white gloves and waited, not expecting her to come in, but she did; I received her and then she bought a basket. Since this we have always had a stall. I have missed only two, one when I was ill and one through what I thought was the meanness of the County Director. That time the Queen was going too, to open a new Market the money for which had been collected by the Thorpe Red Cross Association. They were coming in a private bus, and would, I am sure, have squashed me in by the entrance. But that was that. Two years later I was told I could no longer wear uniform to go in, as I was over age. I wore my 50 years' service badge, though.

The Sandringham Show though much smaller than the Royal Norfolk Show, is much more animated and crowded, and we are busier. Some customers come from as far away as York. So I don't know what I shall do; stay at home, perhaps? If I don't go, I might miss something exciting; after all, the Queen Mother is older than me.

Epilogue

On the 9th January 1995, Jane was 91 years old.
March came in like a lion and there was some snow. The planned expedition to church had been cancelled, and by mid-week Jane was feeling very poorly and the doctor was called. However, on the Saturday morning she seemed to be feeling better. A friend who popped in to see her said she was quite bright and cheerful and sitting up in bed reading the newspaper. Jane died later that morning peacefully in her sleep in the house where she had been born 92 years before.